Counseling
and
Homosexuality

RESOURCES FOR
CHRISTIAN COUNSELING

Counseling and Homosexuality

EARL D. WILSON, Ph.D.

RESOURCES FOR
CHRISTIAN COUNSELING

——————— General Editor ———————

Gary R. Collins, Ph.D.

WORD PUBLISHING
Dallas · London · Vancouver · Melbourne

COUNSELING AND HOMOSEXUALITY, Volume 15 of the Resources for Christian Counseling series. Copyright © 1988 by Word, Incorporated. All rights reserved. No portion of this book may be reproduced in any form, except for brief quotations in reviews, without written permission from the publisher.

Library of Congress Cataloging-in-Publication Data

Wilson, Earl D., 1939–
    Counseling and homosexuality / Earl D. Wilson.
        p.   cm. — (Resources for Christian counseling ; v. 15)
    Bibliography: p.
    Includes index.
    ISBN 0-8499-3615-2
    1. Gays—Pastoral counseling of.   2. Homosexuality—Religious aspects—Christianity.   3. Church work with gays.   I. Title.
    II. Series.
    BV4437.5.W55   1988
    253.5—dc19   88-5749
                                                                      CIP

Printed in the United States of America

4 5 6 7 8 9 LBM 9 8 7 6 5 4 3 2 1

CONTENTS

EDITOR'S PREFACE

IN AN "INTRODUCTION TO COUNSELING" course several years ago, I gave a lecture on homosexuality and was approached after class by a student who wanted to talk. As he shared about the past, my student described his "gay lifestyle" prior to conversion. For several years he had frequented gay bars, had been involved sexually with a number of male partners, and had lived for a while with a lover.

After his conversion, the student's behavior changed but his sexual orientation did not. He was still attracted sexually to men, felt no sexual attraction toward women, and wondered if he still could have a ministry in the church.

We discussed these issues during several meetings and one day the student volunteered to talk about his past experiences and present struggles before the counseling class. The result was electrifying. Before that time, some students had joked about homosexuals or had passed them off as "sinners who ought to stop being gay." But these insensitive attitudes quickly

9

faded when the class members began to glimpse the pain and struggles that many homosexually oriented people face. Before the end of the semester, two or three additional students admitted that they had similar struggles but had never suspected that others, especially some of their fellow classmates and ministerial students, felt the same way.

It is not surprising that homosexually oriented people are in seminaries and probably in positions of Christian leadership. Perhaps there are few student bodies, church congregations, business corporations, or mission societies that don't have at least a few homosexual people among their numbers. If these people are believers, they know that yielding to homosexual lust is as damaging as yielding to heterosexual lust. But for many, especially those who are young, the temptations are strong and the urges are sometimes intense.

In the pages that follow you will meet several people—male and female—who are attracted sexually to persons of the same sex. And you will meet their counselor, a man who shows sensitivity, compassion, and understanding, all combined with a firm commitment to biblical truth and a clear acceptance of the Bible's teaching about homosexuality. Dr. Earl Wilson is a well-trained and highly skilled Christian psychologist whose work with homosexual counselees has given him much of the insight and practical information that he shares with his readers.

When we began the process of selecting authors for the Resources for Christian Counseling series, Earl Wilson was at the top of my list as one who might write on the issue of homosexuality. Dr. Wilson had written previously about sexual problems, and it was encouraging to learn that he would be willing to do an entire book on this one significant sexual issue. With this volume he becomes the first author to write two books in the Resources for Christian Counseling series. (Dr. Wilson also wrote Counseling and Guilt, volume 8.)

All of the books in the series are intended to be practical and helpful. Written by counseling experts, each of whom has a strong Christian commitment and extensive counseling experience, the volumes are intended to be examples of accurate psychology and careful use of Scripture. Each is intended to have a clear evangelical perspective, careful documentation, a strong practical orientation, and be free of the sweeping statements and undocumented rhetoric that sometimes characterize books in the counseling field. Our goal is to provide books that are clearly written, useful, up-to-date overviews of the issues faced by contemporary Christian counselors. All of the Resources for Christian Counseling books have similar bindings and together they are intended to comprise a helpful encyclopedia of Christian counseling.

The author of this book is a seminary teacher and a counseling practitioner whose work often puts him in contact with homosexually oriented people. Too often, it seems, evangelicals are like those students in my introductory counseling class—inclined to be critical and condemning of homosexuality until they meet one or two people who struggle with a sexual orientation that they didn't choose, often do not want, but frequently have difficulty controlling. Dr. Wilson clearly understands these people and knows how to help them.

The recent AIDS epidemic has focused attention on homosexuality. Behavior that may have been ignored or rarely discussed in counseling only a few years ago has now become part of the daily news and probably is encountered with greater frequency by counselors. As you work with homosexually oriented people, this book should be a helpful guide that will increase both your understanding and your counseling effectiveness.

Gary R. Collins, Ph.D.
Kildeer, Illinois

INTRODUCTION

When Gary Collins first contacted me about writing this book I felt a strange mixture of excitement and fear. I was excited because I knew I have something to say and some experiences to share. I was fearful because I knew I was stepping into the battleground of the next decade. I thought about how little is actually known about homosexuality and yet how dogmatic people have become. I thought about prejudice and gay bashing. I thought about people whose lives have been threatened because they dared to say that the practice of homosexuality is a sin. I thought about AIDS. How can anyone not think about that these days? Finally, I thought about the counselees with whom I had worked.

I remembered their tears and their frustration. Gary had said the book must show compassion, and I knew I was okay on that score. Hurting people need our love. I talked to some of my counselees about the book. I asked for permission to tell a part of their stories. Their faith in me inspired me to move forward with the task.

I searched for new research and most of the time found nothing. In its place I found a swamp of opinions through which I reluctantly waded.

I must acknowledge the fact that much of the book is my personal opinion and theory. I do not apologize for that because someone has to take a stand. On the other hand, I will take responsibility for my views and try to handle any criticism which may come in an honest manner.

Now that the work is finished, the emotions of excitement and fear are both still there, but in a weakened form. Hard work dulls excitement; writing the book has been difficult. In like manner, the fear has dissipated as I have grown in my conviction that we as Christian counselors dare not step back from difficult topics.

I have included portions of the stories of a number of my clients. As you would expect, I have changed their names and nonessential details to insure their privacy.

As you read this volume allow yourself to feel with me the mixed emotions that often emerge when we are willing to walk close to those whose needs are great.

CHAPTER ONE

THE NEW WAVE OF UNCERTAINTY

"I DON'T KNOW WHO I AM," Jennifer cried. "I have all these strange feelings inside me and I'm afraid they will come out."

Nick was more bold. "I don't know what is going to happen to me. But I'm tired of living like one person and feeling like another."

Both Jennifer and Nick are struggling with the same uncertainty—the uncertainty of same-sex preference. Their patterns of sexual arousal are oriented toward persons of the same sex and they experience little or no attraction to the opposite sex.

Nick and Jennifer are in two different places with their problem. Jennifer's struggle is within. She hasn't acted upon her confused feelings so there are no entanglements with people and no fears of disease. Nick, on the other hand, has begun to flirt with the dangers of sexual encounters in public places and a constant stream of sexual contact. Neither Nick nor Jennifer wants to give up the Christian faith, but they are finding it increasingly difficult to fit it in. Jennifer is bombarded by a constant stream of guilt. Even though she has not acted upon her impulses she is plagued by a deep feeling that a "true Christian" wouldn't have this type of struggle. Nick is becoming hardened by disobedience. "I'm telling God that I'm going to do things my way," he says, "and it is getting easier all the time. Sometimes I even wonder if I'm a believer." They need help, but they don't know where to turn.

The examples of the lives of Jennifer and Nick only scratch the surface of the millions of persons who struggle with homosexuality. Many of this number are religious or profess to be Christians. They are in our churches, our youth organizations, and our Christian homes. They cannot be ignored. They must be understood and ministered to.

Socially they represent one of the emerging subcultures of our time. They have social needs and the political clout to see that those social needs are met. They are a diverse group, yet bound together by a common struggle. Personally, they often experience feelings of loneliness, isolation, and fear of never belonging. They often have experienced rejection by parents and abandonment by peers. With the increased fear of AIDS, they are often feared and shunned. They seek understanding and compassion only to find confusion and lack of concern.

HOMOSEXUALITY: A PERSONAL AND POLITICAL DILEMMA

Whenever the word *homosexuality* is used, emotions are stirred and opinions are ventured. It is a subject about which it is hard to be neutral. Homosexuality has become one of the hottest social issues in the decade of the eighties and has the potential to spark revolution in the nineties. Concerns which begin as personal-quality issues and style-of-life issues for the individual struggling with same-sex preference, turn to social, theological, and political battles when they are considered in the broader context.

John R. W. Stott has written regarding the challenge that homosexuality presents for the church and for theologians,

The secular world says: "Sex is essential to human fulfillment. To expect homosexual people to abstain from homosexual practice is to condemn them to frustration and to drive them to neurosis, despair and even suicide. It's 'inhuman and inhumane' to ask anybody to deny himself what to him is a normal and natural mode of sexual expression. Indeed, it's positively cruel."

But no, the Word of God teaches that sexual experience is not essential to human fulfillment. To be sure, it is a good gift of God. But it is not given to all, and it is not indispensable to humanness. Jesus Christ was single, yet perfect in his humanity. God's commands are good and not grievous. The yoke of Christ brings rest not turmoil; conflict comes only to those who resist it.

So ultimately it is a crisis of faith: Whom shall we believe? God or the world? Shall we submit to the lordship of Jesus, or succumb to the pressures of prevailing culture? The true "orientation" of Christians is not what we are by constitution, but what we are by choice.[1]

Homosexuals are no longer just "those people over there." They are our neighbors. They are our fellow church members. They are our families. In essence they are us. We can no longer escape the problem.

The sharp increase in identified homosexuals, coupled with the widespread publicity of the deadly disease called AIDS, has resulted in a new word: "homophobia."

Sam's case may help us to get both sides of the story. He wasn't looking for controversy, but he found it. On the other hand, he was looking for friends, vocational and social gratification, and sexual fulfillment, but these things eluded him.

Sam was the first-born son of an upper middle-class family in Southern California. His father was a highly successful businessman whom people said "knows how to get things done." Sam's mother was critical and angry and resented her husband being gone so much. Sam was just a regular child until about the time he entered school. He liked adults better than children and he liked to play house with the neighbor girls more than he liked to play soccer or football. He was a little frail and cried a lot. This often angered his father, and his mother withdrew because "my nerves just couldn't take it." Sam's father criticized the mother for letting Sam be a sissy, but she replied, "As long as he is happy I'm not going to rock the boat." However, at the same time she was pushing Sam toward perfectionism. "Anything that is worth doing is worth doing well," she was heard to say.

Sam felt more and more isolated and more and more strange as his life continued. By the time he was in the third grade he knew he was different but he didn't know why. He spent more and more time reading and listening to music. He didn't learn to play baseball because his dad was too busy and he was afraid to try to learn it on his own with the other kids. By the time he reached junior high school he didn't have many friends and he was afraid to compete in sports. His world became more and more narrow.

When Sam was in high school he had his first homosexual encounter. He had oral sex with a neighbor man who had befriended him. This led to feelings of guilt and fear that his father would discover his activity. This fear led to a period of abstinence although Sam's thoughts were turning more and more to men. He became a Christian during high school and secretly hoped that God would take the sexual temptation away. But this did not happen and the agony continued.

By the time Sam was a sophomore in college he could no longer resist the temptation and "came out of the closet" into an active homosexual lifestyle. His parents withdrew from him and he was alone, except for his homosexual friends. Although he still believed in God, his Christian life was on hold and he had dropped out of any type of Christian fellowship. Sam was alone. He was not satisfied with his sex life. (He felt guilty being content.) He was afraid of not being able to get a job if people found out about his sexual orientation and he needed friends desperately. His homosexual contacts were not meeting the needs in that area.

In desperation, Sam returned to church, hoping to find

acceptance, fellowship, and the opportunity to use the gifts
God had given him. Instead, his presence was met with fear
and rumors of his gay lifestyle. Once again he was met with a
sign that said "Dead End." At this point he moved from the
area and sought counseling. He too feared AIDS and he feared
God's wrath; but he couldn't find a way out. He said, "I feel
trapped. I can't be happy as a gay and I don't seem to be able
to figure out how to live as a straight." His life seemed to be
total despair, interrupted by only brief moments of sexual
pleasure, followed by extreme loneliness and guilt, which led
to more despair.

The Problem Is a Problem for Christianity

Sam's case is not atypical. Of the thousands of persons who
claim to be homosexual, a significant number are believers.
Although figures are not available regarding the religious orientation of these people, indications are that many, many
homosexuals are committed Christians. These persons are
wandering in and out of our churches looking for peace and
acceptance and trying to figure out what to do with their
lives. Some seek counseling and thus far we have not been
very effective in knowing how to help them. Some in the
church say, "Help them to change." Others say, "They can't
change—help them adjust to how they are." Differences of
opinion such as this have divided people and churches and
have led to brother turning against brother.

Politically, the so-called "gay rights movement" is strong and
getting stronger. Its major tenet is that "gays" should come out
of the closet, accept who they are and be proud of it, and demand the rights that they have as human beings. This stance
is directly opposed by the Christian right-wing politicians
who believe that homosexuality is a choice and that it is not
discrimination to let people live with the consequences of their
choices. In the process of the argument, human compassion is
at times deserted by both sides.

The Battle for the Person

The impact of homosexuality cannot be understood by simply
looking at statistics or social configurations. The heart of the

issue is the human heart. The battle is for the person. If we consider the issue of homosexuality and counseling with homosexuals apart from a strong awareness that we are dealing with real, live people we will err.

Consider, if you will, a person standing in a downtown delicatessen waiting to buy a sandwich for lunch. The person is a Christian—and a practicing homosexual. The gay rights movement wants him. This movement says, "Come join us." He is not totally comfortable there because they do not understand his Christian values. But they do invite him to come join them.

The church, on the other hand, says nothing. The church does not understand the person and even doubts the Christian commitment. There is no bond formed because basic trust is not there. Where will the person go? Will he seek solace with those who say "come join us—your God made you this way. Surely he doesn't want you to be lonely"? Or will the person brave the criticism and fear of the church? Will he dare tell them? Will he dare ask for prayer? Will he share with them his struggle? Will he tell them he wants to be normal, but he just can't be? Which way will he go? He cannot stand in the safety of the deli forever. He has to go home, but where will a home be found?

At the center of the battle for the person is the difficult question, can homosexuals change?

This question also divides people. Recently, a pastor said to me, "I have never known a person who was a true homosexual to change and be happily adjusted as a heterosexual." Many people believe this way. I do not. If I did not believe that it is possible for a homosexual to change I would not be writing this volume. On the other hand, I am not convinced that all homosexuals can change. I believe that to be consistent with Scripture some may have to choose celibacy.

Those who say that all homosexuality is physiological and further imply that God "made them that way" are also wrong. I have taken too many histories and have seen too much evidence to the contrary. Both biblical and scientific data challenge this position.

I believe the gay rights movement is asking people to sell their souls. Homosexuality has little to offer people that is good. As one person said, "I sure hope I don't have to stay this way because it is miserable. I am mistreated by both gays and straights. I have no hope of having the joys of a family. And most of my 'sexual relationships' are not relationships at all." The gay-rights appeal in the battle for the person is an appeal of those in misery who want company. They believe and have demonstrated that there is power in numbers. If thousands believe that the practice of homosexuality is their God-given right then how can they be wrong? The answer—easy! The number of people believing a lie has never been sufficient to turn it into the truth.

If the battle for the person is going to be won, we must offer hope—hope for change for those who want to do so; hope for acceptance and support for those who do not believe they can change. A friend who is a homosexual said, "Until I began to talk to you I believed that the only thing in life for me was the gay lifestyle. Yet, when I practiced it I was miserable. I wanted permanent relationships and all I could find was anonymous sex. I was sick of it and I was tired of living like a hypocrite. Now I feel there is hope. I don't know how much I can change. I don't know if I will ever marry and have children. I don't know how long the struggle with homosexual lust will continue, but I know there is hope. I have begun to change and I'm not giving up until I have taken it as far as it will go."

There is no peace for those in the gay rights movement. They are caught in a struggle for survival. They are faced daily with threats from those who fear and oppose them. They are also faced with the personal threat of not being attractive, as well as the medical threat of disease and death. We nonhomosexuals are much too simplistic in our analysis of their situation. We try to be helpful, with such ridiculous statements as, "Why don't they just stop? They should trust God!" Or, "All they need to do is come to Christ." These and other statements like them fall into the category of true, but not very helpful.

I have dealt with dozens of homosexuals who would like to change but have not known how. I have prayed with those who poured out their heart to God. I have worked with those who have come to Christ. These steps do not take away the problem. Yes, some people have been miraculously delivered

21

from the problem, but there are hundreds and thousands who want deliverance who have not. For these people deliverance comes slowly and painfully and requires learning whole new ways to live. Their greatest need is for loving support during this agonizing process.

THE NAGGING QUESTIONS

The most burning question for those struggling with same-sex preference is *"How did I become this way?"* This large question is followed by a number of lesser ones, all of which reveal the deep agony which the homosexual often experiences. "Is it hormonal? What about genetics? Is it just learned behavior? Can I blame it on my parents? Should I blame it on myself? Why does God let things like this happen? Where do I find the closeness I need?"

The question of causation is a complex one which is often addressed with more emotion than reason. Some ask the question wanting to believe that the condition is temporary and can be changed by a pill or a few counseling sessions. For others the concern is to understand so that they can decide how they want to live their lives. Some ask hoping to be confirmed in their bias; they want a rationalization for continuing in the homosexual lifestyle.

Politically and socially, tremendous pressure is put on the person with same-sex preference to believe that he or she was born that way and therefore should not fight it. The person is often told, "Don't deny it—that is who you are."

Dan said, "My friends tell me over and over again that I'm the way I am because God made me that way. Somehow I can't accept that. I see them giving up all their dreams in order to pursue a lifestyle based upon brief encounters and the lack of permanent relationships. They tell me that I will find someone for me but I just don't see it. I can't go that way—at least until I have given change a try."

In chapter 4 we will explore in depth the most current research and theory regarding the etiology of homosexuality. Suffice it at this point to say that there is no easy answer. The problem is complex and the causes seem to be multiple. In order to be effective in helping the counselee find answers to the questions the counselor must patiently listen, helping the person sort through the many facets of his or her life which may have a bearing upon the problem.

A second question which those who struggle with homosexuality often ask is, "Is change possible?" Nancy said, "I never wanted to be this way, but I just don't know if I can change." Her friend had confused her even more. Most of those who were gay said, "No, you can't change and you shouldn't even try." There were a few, however, who argued to the contrary. Betty said, "I am changing and you can too." This gave Nancy enough hope to seek counseling, but it left her burdened with fears. "I feel like this is my last chance," she said. "If I can't change now I don't know what I will do."

Eric considered change primarily because he was encouraged by one of his Christian friends. "I believe God can turn your life around," Sarah had told him. "You have too much going for you to just throw it all away." Eric came looking for a miracle. I assured him that I also believe in miracles, but that not everyone who seeks Christian counseling for this problem is able to change. Some, in fact, have chosen celibacy as an alternative to change.

There are conflicting reports regarding change. Some, naively I believe, say that no "true homosexual" reverts back to heterosexuality. Others argue, also naively, that the change rate is very high. My experience is mixed. I have seen many either revert back to heterosexuality or convert to heterosexuality if they have not had that experience. On the other hand, I have counseled with many who did not want to change and did not, or who wanted to change but were not able to do so.

The question of change has several components. What does change really mean? Does it mean to be capable of a successful marriage to a person of the opposite sex? Does it mean never to experience homosexual lust? Does it mean to be able to control the compulsion to devote hours to seeking sexual pleasure homosexually? These questions reveal that change is multifaceted and involves concerns not only about sexual arousal but social skills and self-control as well. Success is often in the eyes of the beholder. I never tell a client who is struggling with same-sex preference that counseling will result in his or her never having to struggle again. This may become true, but I cannot guarantee it.

Just as there are many persons who continue to struggle with heterosexual lust, many also will continue to struggle with homosexual lust even if they gain the ability to respond to persons of the opposite sex. In order to be evaluated, change criteria need to be set in terms of the background and goals of the individual counselees.

Change is possible. Lives are transformed by miracles and by hard work. The challenge for the counselor is to help the counselee to keep an open mind while he or she gains in self-understanding and moves forward in new patterns of behavior.

A CALL FOR COMPASSION

As you read the following chapters which deal with the above questions and many other issues, please keep in mind that we are to have the mind of Christ. He was not soft on sin, but he was lovingly compassionate with sinners. He ate in their homes. He listened to their fears and sorrows, and he healed their sick. Dare we strive to be anything less?

CHAPTER TWO

CONFRONTING YOUR OWN VALUES

IN THE EARLY DEVELOPMENTAL YEARS of professional counseling there was an assumption that the counselor would take a neutral position with the counselee regarding issues of values and morals. In 1943 Dr. Carl Rogers wrote:

> I trust it is clear now why there is no philosophy or belief or set of principles which I could encourage or persuade others to have or hold. I can only try to live by *my* interpretation of the current meaning of *my* experience, and try to give others the permission and freedom to develop their own inward freedom and thus their own meaningful interpretation of their own experience.[1]

Although most would agree that counselors should avoid using their position of power to force their beliefs on counselees, few would argue now that a counselor can or should present himself or herself as valueless.

In his book, *When Someone Asks for Help,* Worthington has written,

> Christian helping, therefore, is helping that is done by a Christian who adheres to Christian assumptions, who relies on Christ as the center of the helping relationship and who uses whatever knowledge God has revealed.[2]

This statement emphasizes the importance of the counseling relationship if people are going to be helped to change. When you relate to a counselee you are not a robot or a tabula rasa. You are not devoid of opinions or values. You have beliefs, some of which are very strong. You need not hide these. You will not have an honest relationship with your counselees if you do. On the other hand, the counselees do not have to endorse your values to be helped. I have often learned from my counselees and they have learned from me.

LISTENING OPENS UP MANY DOORS

I often lead my counselees to consider new positions and I work hard to understand their beliefs and perceptions—particularly those that are the most foreign to my way of thinking.

Bill, age 26, had radical beliefs when it came to physical fitness. He worked out every day and he kept his body tan by frequent visits to a tanning parlor. It was almost a religion with him. At times I was threatened by his inferences about people who don't take care of their bodies. As he described his daily routine, which was heavily weighted toward fitness and personal grooming, I wanted to tell him that there are other things in life that are important besides our bodies. I controlled my impulses and began to ask him what fitness meant to him, rather than telling him my views. As I did, I discovered that in his homosexual subculture, personal worth was highly tied to physical appearance. He said, "In my world, if you are not good looking you are nothing." I realized that if I had prematurely challenged him about what I considered an unsatisfactory imbalance in his life, the relationship would have been damaged. My lack of understanding would have been clearly demonstrated and the opportunity to get to some of the important issues such as fear of rejection and lack of self-acceptance might have been lost.

My patience paid off and Bill was able to teach me a lot about his world. One day he said, "Do you see why AIDS is not a major concern for me? I'm getting older and my body isn't as attractive as it used to be. Sometimes I feel like it doesn't matter if I die early because by the time I am thirty I'm dead anyway. I won't be attractive to the people that matter to me and I am not sure I can handle the rejection."

Although Bill's thinking was totally foreign to me I needed to learn from him and use my new awareness to help him deal with the emotional upheaval he was feeling. I admit at times I wanted to say, "Knock it off, Bill. This is stupid! You don't have to be a bronze god to be valuable. You are a nice guy. You are intelligent, interesting, and successful." I know now that if I had said those things they would have fallen on deaf ears. Bill would not have believed my words, therefore trust in me would have been lost.

As I continued to work with Bill I discovered that he was already experiencing some value conflicts regarding his obsession with looks. These conflicts were revealed in the following statements: "I've got to be more than a body . . . . I know I can never have lasting relationships based upon the physical alone."

Later, his spiritual concerns came out. "I wonder sometimes if my body isn't an idol. I certainly spend more time with it than I do with God." Both of these issues were issues I wanted to raise with Bill. If I had challenged his early statements, imposing my views, I probably would have lost the opportunity. On the other hand, when he raised the issues in his time he was very receptive to my views.

I have found it very helpful to follow the rule: *Ask them what they value—don't tell them what they should value.* If you are patient your opportunity to influence will come and when it does it will be favorably received instead of rejected.

Don't Be Afraid of Your Values

I believe in values and I believe very strongly in my values. I also believe in sharing my values with others, including my counselees. As my friend Dr. DeLoss Friesen said, "If our values aren't good to live by then why do we have them? If they are good to live by, then why not share them?"[3]

The key is not so much what you believe and what you share but how you share it. For example, I believe a personal relationship with Jesus Christ is essential for salvation and is critical to the resolution of many of life's problems. However, I see many counselees from all walks of life. Some are believers, some are agnostics, some are struggling with religious doubts and disillusionment. If I state my belief declaratively and dogmatically, I may come across as insensitive or offensive. There is a better way.

I often make the following statement and ask the following question, "I sometimes work with persons who are religious or have a personal faith. Is this something that you would see as a resource in your lives?" Their response tells me a lot about where they are. At this point I am sometimes asked, "What are your beliefs?" Now when I tell them they are ready to listen. I will reply something like, "Well, I believe in God and I believe we can know him personally. This belief has helped me to make sense out of my life." I don't push at this point. Later, I want to be heard when I ask the question, "Do you think God might be relevant here?"

I suggest that those who are clearly identified with a belief system—pastors, lay church counselors, and others—be upfront about where they are belief-wise and how they relate their beliefs to their work.

A Jewish couple with whom I was counseling asked, "You are a Christian aren't you?" I said, "Yes, does that concern you?" The husband responded, "No, unless you preach at us or try to convert us." "I won't do that," I said, "but I do reserve the right to talk about personal faith and beliefs as they might be relevant to your situation." They agreed and were even somewhat enthusiastic.

Other clients have even asked me to explain my faith to them. This I am happy to do, but I usually invite them to let me do it on my time, not time they are paying me for. I do not risk being accused of receiving money for sharing my faith.

This brings us to another helpful rule: *Be real but don't be pushy.* As a believer I am convinced that God is interested in the spiritual welfare of my counselees. My job is to be available to God and to follow the opportunities which he opens up. It is a sacred privilege and I try to use it but not abuse it.

Don't Stereotype

There is a third rule that I follow and that is *Don't stereotype!* When you deal with counselees who can be given a label such as "homosexual," there is a tendency to feel that you know what they are like. You may assume that you know who they are as people because you have read about them. Fortunately, nothing could be further from the truth.

In my early counseling career, Janice, a lesbian, set me straight. "You may think you know who I am," she said, "but you don't. You may think I am a person from your textbook. Well, I'm not! I don't know who I am but I resent people thinking that I'm like others, particularly lesbians."

I realized just how right Janice was. Even if a lesbian strongly identifies with other lesbians and says, "You need to understand us," as some have done, I still need to see *her* as an individual. I am to understand a person and counsel in such a way as to be helpful to that person, not to a stereotype of a group of people.

I try not to assume that I understand the person. I want to know that I understand him or her, and this will never happen if I stereotype.

Another rule: *Seek clarification whenever there is any doubt about what the person is trying to communicate.* This is especially crucial when it comes to understanding the person's value system.

Mark said, "I don't know if I want to change or not." He is resistant to change, I said to myself.

29

"Tell me more, Mark," I said out loud.

"I'm afraid I'll fail," he said. "My lust is so strong I don't know whether I can overcome it or not." Later he said, "I really want to change. I just don't know whether I can or not."

My initial evaluation had been wrong. The counseling process would have been hindered if I had continued to jump to conclusions rather than to ask questions to help Mark tell me what he was actually feeling. Further damage would have been done if I had followed the stereotype of the resistant client. I might have become defensive and pushy and the client, fearful of not being able to change, would have felt unsupported or even rejected.

ATTITUDES GET IN THE WAY

Gary Collins has emphasized the importance of attitudes in the process of helping people. He writes,

> In any helping relationship, the personality, values, attitudes, and beliefs of the helper are of primary importance. . . . In counseling, the effective helper tries to see and understand the problem from the helpee's perspective. "Why is he so upset?" we might ask. "How does he view the situation?" "If I were him, how would I feel?" As helpers we need to keep our own objective viewpoints intact, but we also need to realize that we can be of greatest help if we can in addition see the problem from the helpee's point of view and can let him know that we understand how he feels and views his situation.[4]

Who I am, which includes my attitudes and values, is more important than my training or my position. My attitudes can either be an asset or they can be a hindrance. Skillful counselors are careful not to let their attitudes get in the way.

Judy, a professed lesbian, had not taken very good care of herself. She was overweight and she did not dress attractively. Her appearance created an attitude problem for me. I have trouble accepting people who are not being all that they can be. It was obvious to me that Judy had the potential to be much more attractive than she was. My attitude was negative.

30

This led to another attitude problem. *If she dresses carelessly and she isn't conscientious about her outward self, she probably won't work very hard on her inward self,* I said to myself. By the time my attitude stopped slipping I was convinced that Judy was a bad candidate for counseling and that I should not even waste my time by working with her. The attitude showed and only Judy's boldness saved the counseling relationship.

"You don't like me very much, do you?" she said. I was faced with a moment of truth. I had not faced my lack of acceptance of Judy. "I don't know," I said, "I just realized that so far I have only reacted to your outward appearance and I don't really know who you are. Can we agree that I will try to get to know you, because when I do I may find that I do value you?" She nodded and I realized that we were both more relaxed. The bad attitudes had been taken out of the way.

My rule of thumb regarding counselor attitudes is: *Watch them carefully and deal with them openly when you see them as a hindrance.* What should I as the counselor have done if in the example above I had recognized the problem instead of Judy? I believe the responsible thing to do is to confront yourself first and then if you believe the counselee may have been affected, to confront her or him as well.

Realizing I am feeling critical of Judy I might say to myself, *Okay Earl, give her a chance. Let's see what she is like inwardly.* This could free me to attend more warmly, listen more carefully, and to develop an attitude of caring rather than criticism. In those cases where I believe my attitude may have been interpreted by the counselee I would take a second step as follows. "Judy," I might say, "I feel like I may have set some barriers between us. Is that my problem or do you feel that way also?" I will then follow her response. If she says *no* then I would continue: "That's good because I want to get to know you and be as helpful as I can be." If she said, "I do feel like you don't like me," I would explore her feelings more carefully. "Can you tell me more?" I might ask. At that point she may or may not be able to articulate my critical stare at her clothes and messed-up hair. I have even been so bold as to say, "Maybe I showed some surprise when you came in. I have to admit I was surprised by your appearance. Your telephone voice is very polished and I may have expected that you would dress that way. In any case, let's get to know each other better."

The process I have described may seem laborious to the reader, but I have found that it helps me to keep my attitudes where they need to be and it also helps build good, solid relationships with my counselees. They feel more secure when they realize that I care for them too much to try to cover up bad attitudes or let poor communication put the counseling relationship in jeopardy. At one point Judy said, "Thanks for not just writing me off like most other people do."

AREAS OF SPECIAL CONCERN

There are four areas of concern related to attitudes and values which I believe must be given special attention when counseling—especially with homosexuality.

The first is *prejudice.* "I'm not prejudiced!" I told my wife. "I know you aren't," she replied. "You just have this feeling that you are better than other people." Our interchange took place in a joking manner but both of us knew that there was some truth to the matter. I have rarely met a person who doesn't struggle with prejudice and some of the worst are those of us who disavow that part of our personalities. Differences are rarely seen just as differences. They are usually seen as bad. Differences frighten me. I don't understand so I wish they would go away.

You don't have to be without prejudice to counsel persons with same-sex preference, but you do need to be aware of your prejudice so that you can behave responsibly. I almost never refer to my clients as homosexuals. The word itself stirs up prejudices within me. I gain some control by referring to them as *persons* with same-sex preference. I have no prejudice against persons, in fact I like people very much. This includes people with same-sex preference. I can be more objective seeing the sexual preference as the problem rather than the host of ghosts which may haunt my mind when I think about the word *homosexual.*

Prejudice is usually broken down by getting to know someone who represents that toward which you hold the prejudice. If you focus upon relating to the person and getting to know him or her you will accomplish two important things. You will develop a good counseling relationship and you will change the prejudicial views you hold. Your prejudices will be weakened and your outlook will be more in line with reality.

I remember my first same-sex preference counselee. "This guy's a homosexual," I said to myself. "He must really be weird." I remember being shocked at myself when inwardly I did not want to shake hands with him when he was leaving my office. By the time the second interview was over he no longer seemed weird and I was pleased to note that I was not worried about shaking his hand. At this point we were both more at ease and I was able to extend my energies in helping him deal with his struggles rather than being bogged down in my own.

The rule I apply for myself is as follows. *Consider the persons first.* Get to know them well. You don't have to like or agree with *all that they do but they are people God loves.* Usually when I follow this rule I come to love and care for the person and my counseling is effective.

A second area of special concern is *shock.* This comes in two forms: shock over the type of activities in which the counselees have engaged (Type I), and shock over the persons, some of them prominent religious and civic leaders, who are struggling with the problem (Type II). In most cases shock is usually either an extension of prejudice or lack of social awareness.

The Scripture says "It is shameful even to mention what the disobedient do in secret" (Eph. 5:12), but we know the Lord Jesus himself showed great compassion for those caught in the ironclad trap of sin.

I once asked a counselee who was heavily entrapped in the homosexual scene if he would take me to see some of his world. He said that he would escort me through a gay bar or a leather bar (a bar where specific rituals involving leather are conducted), but he would not take me to the baths (steam baths where multiple sex is common and where there is extensive use of drugs). As I thought about it, I was grateful for his protection of me. In fact, his careful response helped me to realize that there are some things I do not want to see firsthand. I can be satisfied in knowing that they exist without needing to be desensitized to the point of not caring that they exist. The homosexual street scene, like other habitats of open sin, usually contains many dehumanizing elements. I am not shocked when I hear my counselees' involvement in such things, but I am saddened.

One of my counselees had gotten drunk with his "lover" and had fallen into a deep sleep. When he awoke his genital area had been shaved and the other man made fun of him openly. He was humiliated and fearful that I would reject him. He only told me because he was so hurt and depressed by the incident that he had to tell someone. The acceptance and empathy that I was able to extend at this point was a major factor in my counselee's decision to leave that scene and to begin to develop relationships of dignity and respect. Although I often joked with this counselee I never joked about this incident. The hurt was just too great.

In discussing counselee behavior and counselor shock with my students I remind them of one counselor who reacted to a counselee by screaming, "You did WHAT!!?" Both she and the counselee were embarrassed. The student apologized and was somewhat relieved when the counselee said, "It is shocking to me too. Sometimes I cry when I realize how far my behavior is from who I really want to be." My student, sobered and shaken, said, "I'm glad you told me. I don't want to be your judge. It sounds like you do enough of that for yourself. I do want to know where you are so I can help you get where you want to be."

This response illustrates my rule for dealing with shock Type I: *Remember that many bad things happen to people and that people do self-destructive things. They need help, not judgment.*

Type II shock, shock caused by a realization that no one is immune from sin or tragedy, can also be harmful if not overcome. One counselor said, "Not you! How could this happen to you? I've always looked up to you." Unknowingly the counselor was compounding the person's problems. By her shock response she was only adding to the person's guilt and making it more difficult for the woman to remain in the counseling relationship.

In a similar situation the shocked counselor had more

control. "Take your time and tell me whatever you want to say," he said. "I know this must be difficult for you." The counselee began to sob silently, then said, "I've ruined everything. I'm a disgrace to my family and I am a shame to God." The counselor was able to work with the person in search of a hopeful solution because the shock was overcome. Is it any wonder that when writing about restoring a brother taken in sin the apostle Paul wrote,

> Brothers, if someone is caught in a sin, you who are spiritual should restore him gently. But watch yourself, or you also may be tempted. Carry each other's burdens, and in this way you will fulfill the law of Christ.   (Gal. 6:1, 2)

The rule I apply for Type II shock is: *Remember that sin and suffering are not respecters of persons and neither is God. He wants to give healing to all.*

Don't stand in awe of the counselees who come to you for help. Regardless of their status, high or low, they are there because they need you or the help you can find for them. Stand by them and you will find that you can make a difference.

Another special concern is *homophobia*. By this term I mean a fear of homosexuals or of the effects of homosexuality. Here are some examples of the problem. A deacon said, "We can't have homosexuals in our church. They will corrupt our youth." Matt, a young counselor, said, "Is it dangerous to counsel 'them'?" A homosexual client who himself suffered from homophobia asked, "What about touching my sons? Are they going to be hurt by me?"

When it comes to fears, we often fear most the things we do not understand. If your understanding of homosexuality is limited, you may be reluctant to get involved counseling homosexuals or you may be fearful of relating to them. Some people are afraid that if it is known that they counsel homosexuals they will be stigmatized. I am challenged that Jesus was never afraid of such stigma. He ate with publicans (tax collectors) and sinners. He talked to persons who were demon-possessed and he even spent time talking to a single lady, Mary Magdalene, who had been a prostitute. He wasn't worried about catching their diseases and he wasn't worried about being corrupted by their morals.

In attacking homophobia I am not suggesting that we be naive in our approach. I do not want a practicing homosexual teaching my children. On the other hand, I also do not want my children to be under the influence of a nonrepentant heterosexual sinner, a drug pusher, or a negative person who constantly gossips or tears other persons down. Any of these problems could be negative and I would like to see them avoided whenever possible.

When it comes to worry about AIDS or other sexually transmitted diseases, medically guided caution should be taken. I don't kiss clients and I don't drink out of other people's cups. I have avoided colds and the flu as well as other more dangerous problems. On the other hand, if I am worried about getting AIDS from doorknobs I will be afraid to enter any public building. In short, the best cure for homophobia is realism. There may be individual situations where moral corruption, social influence, or disease should be carefully avoided. This does not mean that I should avoid homosexuals or refuse to invite one home for dinner.

After saying all this I must admit that I myself have a homophobia. I am afraid that the gay rights movement and other forces will be successful in convincing homosexuals that God made them that way and they shouldn't seek to change. This attitude which will come up occasionally throughout the book means I am afraid of homosexuality as a militant social force. I feel it is destructive to the persons with same-sex preference who are involved and may cause many who are in a state of sexual confusion to take on the labels of homosexual or gay when they don't even apply.

The rule for homophobia is quite simple. *Be realistic! Don't run away from people or situations that won't hurt you.*

In general, I have found persons with same-sex preference to be sensitive, caring people. They usually have suffered a lot themselves and few whom I have encountered have any interest in bringing suffering to others.

The final special concern I call *personal sexual threat.* Most people have had the experience of feeling attracted to a person of the same sex at one time or another and have wondered if they themselves could be latently homosexual. If this has been your experience, you may find that you are uncomfortable when you talk with a person for whom this is an ongoing problem. Others who counsel recognize that because of the verbal intimacy associated with counseling they may feel drawn to the person. They may even experience body sensations, which could be interpreted as sexual. If so, you will feel threatened. Usually these feelings pass quickly because they are filtered out by messages from our brains which say, "Forget it—you aren't attracted to the same sex." Listen to these messages. They are right. Focus upon the positive aspects of your sexual adjustment and the threat will pass. Even if it should prove to be a real threat you can handle it by refusing to involve yourself in any sexual way with your client.

I have discussed this issue with same-sex preference counselees who say they are really careful because they don't want to get involved with pastors or friends. The threat is usually more of a problem for the counselor than it is for the counselee.

All counseling involves sexual threat for the counselor because counseling is a very intimate business. That need not deter you, however, if you can apply the following simple but lengthy rule: *Be responsible for your feelings. Realize that just because your feelings may be confused or inappropriate you don't have to act upon them. God wants you to take charge of the feelings rather than give them control over you.*

I admired Don so much I was afraid my admiration would be interpreted as a "come on." A friend in whom I confided was very helpful. He said, "You just take care of yourself. Don sounds like the kind of person who will take care of himself."

WORKING WITHIN YOUR OWN VALUE SYSTEM

Any time you are working with counselees whose behavior and/or values differ significantly from yours, you have to make some decisions about the motive of the relationship. You do not have to counsel all people and you do not have to sacrifice your own values to counsel.

I have a rule which has cost me some clients. I will not counsel a sexual offender if the offense has not been made public. I demand that it be reported to the family and the law. This seems harsh but my experience has shown that sexual offenders who have not come to grips with the legal aspects of their behavior as well as the social and moral aspects usually don't change. Because I don't want to waste my time and their money I require reporting of the abuse, although the law does not demand that I do. I am simply being true to myself and what I believe to be in the best interest of my prospective counselee and society.

Some counselors choose not to work at helping same-sex preference counselees to be better adjusted if the counselees are not willing to either revert back to heterosexuality or convert to heterosexuality if their preference is not in that direction. I have not yet taken that position because I am not sure I can demand those options of all people. I also feel that by staying with the counselees I may eventually lead them to new decisions which they may not be ready for during the early counseling. In some cases where the counselee persisted in self-destructive behavior and seemed not to be helped in any way by my counseling, I terminated the relationship.

Just as you have a responsibility to deal openly with your values with your counselee, you must also be open and honest with yourself. My rule at this point is: *If you cannot come up with goals which are mutually acceptable to you and the client then you should terminate the counseling relationship.*

Counseling, like other types of Christian service, carries with it a solemn responsibility. This responsibility is to know yourself and to be honest with yourself and others. If you do so you may be successful. If you avoid the responsibility you may reap havoc for both yourself and your counselee.

CHAPTER THREE

BIBLICAL CONTROVERSIES REGARDING HOMOSEXUALITY

IN THE PAST TWO DECADES the controversies regarding homosexuality and the Bible have really heated up. Those who support the Gay Christian Movement in the United Kingdom and church bodies such as the Metropolitan Community Church have taken the point of view that the Bible does not condemn the practice of homosexuality. Those with more traditional positions argue that homosexuality is indeed a sin and must be recognized as such.

Richard Lovelace writes:

Until recently, the public posture of all sectors of the church toward homosexuality, even including liberal

39

Protestantism, has rarely diverged from the traditional, negative stance. Homosexuals have been (at least theoretically) welcome in the church if they are repentant and sexually inactive, but active homosexuality has been regarded either as sin or, at the least, as a contagious illness. In the last several decades, however, a number of events have occurred which have raised questions about the church's traditional approach. . . . [1]

In their controversial book *Is the Homosexual My Neighbor?* Scanzoni and Mollenkott suggest that the Bible does not speak about the issue of the homosexual condition, although it may speak about homosexual acts. They write,

Since the Bible is silent about the homosexual condition, those who want to understand it must rely on the findings of modern behavioral science research and on the testimony of those persons who are themselves homosexual.[2]

This view is strongly challenged by many evangelicals who feel that God has addressed the topic and that Scripture has something authoritative to say. Bahnsen writes,

Differing attitudes toward homosexuality within the professing Christian church can often be traced to conflicting views of Scripture. Many disputes over the morality of homosexuality turn on another question: will Scripture be the Christian's normative guide or must it yield that position of authority over ethics to modern scholarship, personal experience, natural reason, new mystical insights, public opinion, or some other standard? The twentieth century has proved to be an age of increasing doctrinal permissiveness among professing Christian teachers: this trend emerged from the modernist abandonment of the absolute authority of God's revealed Word in the Old and New Testaments. Contrary to Scripture's own self-witness as God's inspired and infallible Word, many churchmen have attempted to synthesize Christian commitment with humanistic or secular perspectives in philosophy and the sciences. Throughout the theological spectrum the effect has been distortions of the Christian message that are evident to any thoughtful student.[3]

The position taken by Scanzoni and Mollenkott seems quite risky at best. They are suggesting that an understanding of the homosexual condition requires that one rule out biblical statements as inadequate or too confusing and rely on behavioral science research and personal testimonies. This leaves us with a major problem or two. First, behavioral science research is very controversial and inconclusive as chapter 4 will point out. Secondly, the personal views and testimonies of those who experience the homosexual condition are contradictory and confusing.

There is also confusion across these two categories. While some homosexuals testify to the beauty of what is sometimes called "cohumanity" (homosexual marriage), and scholars write about it in glowing terms, there are definitely differences of opinion. Note the contrasting opinions in the following quotes.

Once sex is no longer confined to procreative genital acts and masculinity and femininity are exposed as social ideologies, then it is no longer possible to argue that sex/love between two persons of the same sex cannot be a valid embrace of bodily selves expressing love. If sex/love is centered primarily on communion between two persons rather than on biological concepts of procreative complementarity, then the love of two persons of the same sex need be no less than that of two persons of the opposite sex. Nor need their experience of ecstatic bodily communion be less valuable.[4]

Sociologist Dennis Altman states a different view:

While the idea that all lesbians seek totally monogamous relationships while all gay men reject monogamy is clearly a myth, it does seem clear that among gay men a long-lasting *monogamous* relationship is almost unknown. Indeed both gay women and gay men tend to be involved in what might be called multiple relationships, though of somewhat different kinds.[5]

Observing these contradictory points of view and many others which could be highlighted from both the behavioral sciences and personal testimony, it would appear that the Scanzoni and Mollenkott expectation of clarification from modern scholarly input will not be realized. Just as the behavioral sciences must face the problem of the bias of the researchers so must the field of biblical interpretation. People tend to see what they want to see. Shall the blind lead the blind or is there at least some light to be followed?

Volumes have been written in attempts to bring clarity to the questions of biblical interpretation. After study of these writings, University of Chicago Professor Robin Scroggs has concluded that there are basically six different positions which scholars take. Four of these positions claim the Bible opposes homosexuality while the other two claim the Bible does not oppose homosexuality.

He summarized these positions as follows.

The Bible Opposes Homosexuality

1. The Bible opposes homosexuality and is definite for what the Church should think and do about it.
2. The Bible opposes homosexuality, but it is just one sin among many. There is no justification for singling it out as more serious than other sins castigated in the Bible, but because of which ordination is not denied.
3. The Bible opposes homosexuality but the specific injunctions must be placed in the larger biblical context of the theology of creation, sin, judgment, and grace.
4. The Bible opposes homosexuality but is so time- and culture-bound that its injunctions may and should be discarded if other considerations suggest better alternatives.

The Bible Does Not Oppose Homosexuality

1. The Bible does not oppose homosexuality because it does not speak of true or innate homosexuality but

42

rather of homosexual acts by people who are not homosexuals.
2. The Bible does not oppose homosexuality because the
    texts do not deal with homosexuality in general.[6]

Having illustrated some of the difficult controversies regarding the Bible and homosexuality, and having highlighted
the various positions taken, we will now devote the remainder
of the chapter to four other important considerations: nonlit-
erary factors affecting interpretation, some key issues in biblical interpretation, the impossibility of changing people's
minds and the necessity for the counselor to know what he or
she believes.

NONLITERARY FACTORS AFFECTING INTERPRETATION

Like many other debates over biblical interpretation the issues are often clouded by biases, distractions, or assumptions
which may have nothing to do with sound exegesis or with the
original languages in which the Bible was written. Two
prominent distractions come up repeatedly in the biblical debates. These are the discussion of inversion versus perversion,
and the distinction between casual and committed sexual relationships. It should be noted at the outset that the Bible does
not discuss either of these topics directly. They are the prod-
ucts of the minds of the interpreter.

Inversion versus Perversion

The distinction between inversion (the acting out of a so-
called innate tendency toward sexual preference for persons of
the same sex) and perversion (the performance of homosexual
acts by persons who are basically heterosexual) was first made
by D. Sherwin Bailey in 1955. His book has become the starting place for those who reject a more literal interpretation of
the Scriptures related to homosexuality. Regarding this distinction, Lovelace writes,

Bailey suggests several lines of argument which have become standard features of later homophile Christian
apologetics. He distinguishes between *perversion,* in

43

which constitutionally heterosexual persons turn their urges toward the same sex in a licentious search for thrills, and *inversion*, the constitutional preference for the same sex felt by exclusive homosexuals. It is significant that in order to maintain this distinction he rules out the several degrees of bisexuality recognized by Kinsey.[9] Bailey contends that the biblical passages dealing with homosexual acts, including the three principal texts in the New Testament which he acknowledges as referring to these practices (Romans 1:27; 1 Corinthians 6:9, 10; and 1 Timothy 1:9, 10), deal with perversion, not with inversion, so that in effect the biblical witness is irrelevant to what he would consider responsible and loving homosexual conduct.[7]

The argument seems to become very circular. If it is natural, it is right. If it is occurring in other than the perverted sense, it is natural so it must be right. If it is right or unavoidable, it must not be condemned. Only the homosexual acts of the person who is not a true homosexual must be condemned. These are the so-called "unnatural acts."

David Fields sounds a well-taken word of caution regarding this kind of thinking. He says:

> But doubts about causation must not be allowed to obscure the ethical significance of homosexual inversion. Those who have never known any physical attraction for the opposite sex can hardly be blamed for their condition. It seems self-evident that to reproach a practicing invert for behaving "unnaturally" is nonsensical. Is it not therefore right for the Christian moralist to condone the invert's homosexual life-style—in the interests of understanding and compassion—while remaining absolutely adamant in condemning the pervert?[8]

Casual versus Committed Relationships

The second distinction which often clouds the issue of biblical interpretation is the distinction between casual and committed relationships. The argument is that the Bible encourages committed relationships while condemning casual relationships, such as sex outside of marriage. Therefore if a relationship, even homosexual in nature, is a committed relationship, we dare not assume that it is wrong or condemned by God. Most writers, both conservative and liberal, argue that casual homosexual relationships are wrong. The notion of a committed homosexual relationship as the equivalent to marriage is intriguing to our compassionate sides, but the fact remains that Scripture is silent on the topic. Scanzoni and Mollenkott bring the issue into sharp focus.

The Bible, furthermore, does not mention the possibility of a permanent, committed relationship of love between homosexuals analogous to heterosexual marriage. Surely, such a union is to be distinguished from the contexts we have looked at, contexts of violence, idolatry, and lust. But would such a relationship be permissible according to biblical standards? Or do theological considerations such as God's plan in creating male and female and bringing them together to be "one flesh" rule out homosexual unions entirely?[9]

By making the highly questionable assumption that biblical silence is to be equated with permission or positive sanction, Scanzoni and Mollenkott free themselves to return to the hallmark of situational ethics, "If it is loving it is right."

Where Do We Stand?

In reviewing the distinctions cited above it is clear that the issues of biblical interpretation have been taken from the language scholars and the exegetes and have been subjected to matters of philosophy, modern ethics, and world view. The extreme to which this position can take us can be seen in the following quote from Thomas Maurer who rejects anything traditional.

Why don't we have the courage and the candor to admit that the attitudes and opinions expressed by these ancient writers are thoroughly reprehensible and repugnant? . . .

What in the world is a twentieth-century theologian doing trying to interpret the doctrine of original sin so that it can be made less damning of man in general and of the homosexual in particular? . . . To be valid, a theology has to be created out of one's own experience, out of one's own visceral being. . . . There is no greater misuse of the Bible than to make it our taskmaster, a body of writing to which we are enslaved. I can see no validity whatsoever to the claim that something written two or three thousand years ago has any special relevance to my way of living and thinking. I happen to buy most of what Jesus said, but not because it's in the Bible or because he said it, but rather because I find it existentially valid. And I have to be candid enough to say that there are a few things Jesus said that I can't buy.[10]

It seems apparent that those who seek to interpret Scripture literally without the distinctions which may be used to explain away the intended meaning will be seen as both antischolarly and antihomosexual. This schism, although not new, is most unfortunate and offers little hope for either scholarship or the homosexual struggler. Just as hatred supported by biblical authority is not the answer, neither is love based upon acceptance of standards which are offensive to God and destructive to both the individual and society.

KEY ISSUES IN BIBLICAL INTERPRETATION

As an educator trained in both theology and the social sciences I find it curious to see how biblical texts are viewed by people in the two fields. Masters and Johnson, whose training is in medicine and psychiatry and whose interest and research is in human sexuality, apparently have little trouble with biblical interpretation. They write,

Homosexuality was clearly condemned in the earliest Jewish tradition. In the Bible we are told: "And if a man lie with mankind, as with womankind, both of them have committed abomination: they shall surely be put to death; their blood shall be upon them" (Leviticus 20:13).[11]

46

The Analogy of Faith

In my beginning course in biblical interpretation I was taught a basic principle called the analogy of faith. In essence, the principle states that any interpretation must take into account the entire teaching of scripture. The assumption is that there is unity within Scripture and the Bible is its own best commentary. Following this principle, specific interpretations of the passages which refer to homosexuality would best be accomplished by taking into account the teaching of the entire Bible regarding sexuality. This idea is supported by Don Williams, who writes,

> When turning to the Bible for its understanding of homosexuality we must not jump in at any point which we choose. We must begin where the Bible begins: "In the beginning God. . . ." This becomes a critical point for us. The modern interpreters who claim that the Bible is not opposed to homosexuality *per se* start, not with the opening chapters of Genesis "the beginning," but with the account of Sodom and Gomorrah. This is true of D. S. Bailey, Robert Treese, and John McNeill.[12]

Biblical interpreters such as those cited by Williams deny that the orderliness of the creation, specifically the creation of males and females and the command to become one flesh, has anything to do with understanding homosexuality. Such is not the case. Williams further asserts:

> Man has been created as the pinnacle or center of creation to participate in God's ordering of the world. This includes the ordering of the sexes as male and female. To break this order is to create disorder, to turn from cosmos to chaos.
>
> Furthermore, procreation is only secondary to the original intention of creating male and female for community in both Genesis 1 and Genesis 2. Therefore the unity of the two sexes cannot be overturned as merely a justification for their sexual relationship in creation which has now been

47

transcended in redemption. Something more essential is at stake here: the reflection of the image of God through Man as male and female together. This unity of the sexes is then extended to their sexual relationship in the special command to be fruitful and multiply. Needless to say, a homosexual relationship is unable to fulfill that command. This leads us to suspect that this inability is a result of an improper ground. Man is designed to live together as male and female, nothing else fulfills God's will.[13]

Read the Text—Not Between the Lines

The necessity of looking at what is said, and not just searching for what is omitted in Scripture, cannot be stated too strongly. Although words may be a source of confusion they also straighten out a lot of confusion if taken at face value.

Let's take Romans chapter 1 as an example. What does it say?

Although they claimed to be wise, they became fools and exchanged the glory of the immortal God for images made to look like mortal man and birds and animals and reptiles. Therefore God gave them over in the sinful desires of their hearts to sexual impurity for the degrading of their bodies with one another. They exchanged the truth of God for a lie, and worshiped and served created things rather than the Creator—who is forever praised. Amen. Because of this, God gave them over to shameful lusts. Even their women exchanged natural relations for unnatural ones. In the same way the men also abandoned natural relations with women and were inflamed with lust for one another. Men committed indecent acts with other men, and received in themselves the due penalty for their perversion.   (Rom. 1:22–27)

It says that men lusting after men is shameful, just as Leviticus 20:13 declares that to lie with a person of the same sex is an abomination. It seems obvious that if "God created certain persons to be homosexual"[14] as Troy Perry asserts, then these verses would surely have included an exception clause for the sake of the righteous homosexuals.

A similar conclusion can be drawn by reading the New Testament passages regarding marriage. If marriage is acceptable for persons of the same sex, then why does 1 Corinthians 7:2 emphasize only the husband and wife relationship as a means of avoiding immorality?

But since there is so much immorality, each man should have his own wife, and each woman her own husband. The husband should fulfill his marital duty to his wife, and likewise the wife to her husband. The wife's body does not belong to her alone but also to her husband. In the same way, the husband's body does not belong to him alone but also to his wife. Do not deprive each other except by mutual consent and for a time, so that you may devote yourselves to prayer. Then come together again so that Satan will not tempt you because of your lack of self-control. I say this as a concession, not as a command. I wish that all men were as I am. But each man has his own gift from God; one has this gift, another has that. (1 Cor. 7:2–7)

I agree with the conclusion Greenlee reaches with regard to this passage.

The language of 1 Corinthians 7:2 implies exclusiveness. It is impossible to find in Paul's words here any room for other types of relationships than that of husband and wife. This passage cannot mean, "Let each man have his own wife or male bed-companion (*koinolektros*) and each woman have her own husband or female bed-companion." In these verses Paul recognizes celibacy as a legitimate life style and then recommends marriage (male-female) as a safer course. Why does he not admit the additional option of a homosexual union? Such relations were well known and practiced in Corinth and they probably could more readily have been made respectable in the Christian community of Corinth than in many other localities. If mere avoidance of sexual promiscuity was Paul's concern, a settled homosexual union would have served that purpose as well as heterosexual marriage. It is clear, then, that Paul did not consider a homosexual union a legitimate option for a Christian. There is no sufficient reason for his failing to include such an option in a passage such as this if he had considered same-sex unions proper.[15]

Biblical Arguments Must Take Precedence Over Personal Experience

Who could deny that homosexuals are lonely and hurting people? Who would deny that the church has a responsibility to minister to them? The real question is, do we have to interpret the Bible differently to do so? I think not. In fact, I believe to rationalize any human problem may deny the afflicted the opportunity to find true relief. If homosexuality is sin and sin separates us from God, then to rationalize sin is ultimately to deny the homosexual access to God and healing. Bonhoeffer called for a return to Scripture in his day and surely such a call is timely now.

We must learn to know the Scriptures again, as the Reformers and our fathers knew them. We must not grudge the time and the work that it takes. . . . How, for example, shall we ever attain certainty and confidence in our personal and church activity if we do not stand on solid Biblical ground? It is not our heart that determines our course, but God's Word. But who in this day has any proper understanding of the need for scriptural proof? How often we hear innumerable arguments "from life" and "from experience" put forward as the basis for most crucial decisions, but the argument of Scripture is missing. And this authority would perhaps point in exactly the opposite direction. It is not surprising, of course, that the person who attempts to cast discredit upon their wisdom should be the one who himself does not seriously read, know, and study the Scriptures.[16]

I feel that the Bible has more to say about homosexuality and heterosexuality than we are willing to read and comply with. We may be in danger of selling our birthrights for porridge and in so doing condemning our homosexual peers (brothers and sisters in Christ) to less than God intended for them.

THE IMPOSSIBILITY OF CHANGING PEOPLE'S MINDS

Many counselors, particularly those with a high view of Scripture, believe that their job is to straighten people out. They sometimes enter the counseling session armed with "the Truth" and intent on changing their counselees, if not the whole world. They fail! It doesn't work. Differences in perception are not changed by logic. Even though I believe that it is truth which ultimately leads to freedom, my experience has shown that telling is not enough.

> To the Jews who had believed him, Jesus said, "If you hold to my teaching, you are really my disciples. Then you will know the truth, and the truth will set you free."
>
> (John 8:31, 32)

We as counselors need to be armed with truth but ready to admit that it is God who must do the convincing. I ask people to consider my point of view but I do not demand that they accept it. I challenge my counselees' beliefs if they appear to be contrary to Scripture, but I do not want to "win the argument and lose the person." I am quick to point out problems in biblical interpretation and I am also quick to recognize the inadequacies of modern science. We need to continually affirm that there are no easy answers.

Often the issues of biblical interpretation hinge on the counselee's belief that he or she cannot change. I concentrate on helping the counselees to keep options open and possibilities out in front of them. Often, as behavior changes so do beliefs. Counselees who see the hope of change are more willing to accept the biblical teachings.

Do not try to overpower your counselee, but at the same time do not become so enamored with science that you yourself forget the Bible.

It is true that biblical interpretation must be reevaluated in the light of new scientific knowledge. Few responsible scientists, however, are as confident about the results of their disciplines as onlooking theologians. New data and hypotheses in psychology, sociology, endocrinology, and medicine can shed new light on our understanding of homosexuality and the church's response to it. But frequently the results of scientific inquiry are tentative and inconclusive, neutral in their theological and ethical implications, or even weighted with unspoken values and assumptions which contradict biblical faith.[17]

COUNSELOR, KNOW WHAT YOU BELIEVE

Counselees will enter your office with a wide variety of fears, conceptions, and misconceptions about counselors and the counseling process. They will ask questions and will not be satisfied unless you have answers. The two most common questions I am asked are: "What do you believe about divorce?" and "Do you believe that homosexuals can change?" On the heels of the latter question I am often asked, "Do you believe that the Bible teaches that homosexuality is sin?"

In most instances I do not answer the questions directly until I have a chance to get to know my counselee better. Usually I state that what I believe is not nearly as important as what they believe because they have to live with their beliefs, not mine. If pressed, I will state my belief that the practice of homosexuality is sin, just as the sexual expression of heterosexuality outside of marriage is sin. I also state clearly that I do not believe that homosexual lust is any worse than heterosexual lust. All lust is sin and we have a responsibility to God to practice self-control in these areas. At this point in the counseling process I try to allow counselees plenty of time to think about what has been said and to compare my position with what they believe.

Some have worked very hard not to believe anything, and will need your help even to think through the issues. Others will be militantly opposed to the stance you take, while still others will criticize you for not going far enough. You cannot win and you should not try to do so. Your goal is to stay in contact with counselees so that you can be of assistance as they

52

strive to reach their goals. Some will choose goals you cannot support. In those instances I usually make referrals to other counselors who will be able to work with them.

One thing I always emphasize is my belief in a God who cares and one who is interested in growth and change. I could not honestly counsel with homosexuals if I did not believe that they can change. I believe there is hope and I extend that hope to the counselees, although I make it clear that there are no guarantees. No guarantees, that is, other than God's abiding love.

CHAPTER FOUR

CAUSES OF HOMOSEXUALITY

IF YOU LIKE DIFFERENCES OF OPINION with very few facts to back them up you will be intrigued by studying causes of homosexuality. For years this study was neglected because the phenomenon was not talked about and even scholars chose to put their efforts in other areas. William Wilson has traced some of the differing views regarding homosexuality, dating back to publications of the 1930s. He writes,

With the development of modern science, the early investigators of homosexuality considered it to have its origin in the physical workings of the body. Both Krafft-Ebing and Havelock-Ellis believed that it had a constitutional, or hereditary, cause. With the development of Freudian dynamic psychiatry, there was an abrupt swing away from this position to one that emphasized early-life experiences as being the primary cause. W. J. Gadpaille has noted that there are two distinct theoretical positions—biological and environmental. According to the first theory, there is an innate biological sexuality and a child's development proceeds through a series of phases representing partial instincts that must ultimately become integrated harmoniously for adult sexual functioning. . . . The second theory, emphasizing environment, finds "a typical family constellation in the background of male homosexuals, consisting of a close binding intimate mother and a detached, indifferent or hostile father. The mother's influence demasculinized the son and stripped the father of admirable masculine qualities, and the father made identification with himself unpalatable."[1]

In the last ten years the controversy over causality has become more intense because of the political pressure of the Gay Rights Movement which asserts strongly that homosexuals are born that way and cannot change. A lead sentence for an article on "Sexual Destinies" in *OMNI* magazine read, "'Homosexuals are born, not made,' claims one physician who says he has proof positive that sexual orientation is sealed in the womb."[2] The article, which focuses upon the work of Dr. Günter Dörner, Director, Institute of Experimental Endocrinology at Humboldt University in East Berlin, summarizes much of the controversy. Dörner is the first scientist who is trying to prove that homosexuality is biologically determined. His work is being met with responses ranging from praise for his courage to skepticism and strong criticism. It is clear that the battle is brewing. The issue of causality is now getting plenty of attention. The results of such attention are yet to be seen.

We will return to ther discussion of biological causality of homosexuality later. At this point, however, we will review other views which also seem to be gaining momentum.

WHAT IS THE STATUS OF FREUD?

Most psychological inquiry seems to take a leap from the ancients to Sigmund Freud. Even early explanations of the causes of homosexuality seem to have landed on Freud's doorstep. Freud focused upon disordered parent-child relations as a potential cause of homosexuality. His clinical observations pointed to a rejecting or hostile mother and a passive father as precursors of the homosexual condition. Collins writes,

> Psychoanalytic theories have maintained that homosexuality comes to males raised in families where there is a weak, passive, ineffective father and a domineering mother. This mother subtly teaches her son to be passive and dedicated to her. He has no strong male example to follow and soon discovers that he is less competent than his peers in relating to girls. The son, therefore, loses confidence in his masculinity and dreads the thought of intimacy with women. Daughters in such families perceive their fathers as being unfriendly or rejecting so the girls have little opportunity to relate to really masculine men. They relate better to women.[3]

This view was accepted for years although there was little but the reputation of Freud to back it up. This position was restated in 1962 by Bieber who wrote,

> The father played an essential and determining role in the homosexual outcome of his son. In the majority of instances the father was explicitly detached and hostile. In only a minority of cases was paternal destructiveness effected through indifference or default.
>
> A fatherless child is deprived of the important paternal contributions to normal development; however, only a few homosexuals in our sample had been fatherless children. Relative absence of the father, necessitated by occupational demands or unusual exigencies, is not in itself pathogenic.
>
> A good father-son relationship and a mother who is an

affectionate, admiring wife, provide the son with the basis for a positive image of the father during periods of separation.

We have come to the conclusion that a constructive, supportive, warmly-related father precludes the possibility of a homosexual son. . . . Most mothers of homosexual sons were possessive of them.[4]

Although this position seems to have face validity and is documented with substantial case material it certainly cannot account for a very high percentage of either homosexuals or lesbians. The majority of the persons I have seen who struggle with same-sex preference have not had rejecting parents of the opposite sex. There are, however, some persons I have seen whose backgrounds would fit into this pattern. I believe this points once again to multiple causality.

MOBERLY'S INTERPRETATION OF PARENT-CHILD RELATIONS

The recent work of Elizabeth Moberly, a British writer, has called new attention to the place of parent-child relations in the homosexual condition, but from a different perspective. Moberly contends that the underlying maladaptive relationship is with the same-sex parent, not the opposite as Bieber and others have contended. Her theory, which is quite complex, suggests both causal factors and suggestions for therapy which are based upon those theoretical considerations. Moberly writes,

It is sometimes asserted that analytic evidence and explanations are too varied to be helpful. It might be truer to say that the phenomenon of homosexuality is more complex and many-faceted than might at first sight be apparent. From amidst a welter of details, one constant underlying principle suggests itself: that the homosexual—whether man or woman—has suffered from some deficit in the relationship with the parent *of the same sex;* and that there is a corresponding drive to make good this deficit—through the medium of same-sex, or "homosexual," relationships.[5]

In detailing her position Moberly points out that the hurt which resulted in a disruption of the attachment of the parent of the same sex may have been deliberate or it may even be unknown by the parent. She also argues that damage may have been done even though the child may have gotten over the situation.

The inability and sometimes unwillingness of the child to relate to the parent of the same sex results in unmet needs which the person seeks to satisfy through persons of the same sex later in life.

Needs for love from, dependency on, and identification with, the parent of the same sex are met through the child's attachment to the parent. If, however, the attachment is disrupted, the needs that are normally met through the medium of such an attachment remain unmet. Not merely is there a disruption of attachment, but further, a defensive detachment. This resistance to the restoration of attachment (in analytic terms, counter-cathexis and not the mere withdrawal of cathexis) is what marks the abiding defect in the person's actual relational capacity, that long outlasts the initial occasion of trauma. However, the repression of the normal need for attachment has to contend, like every repression, with the corresponding drive towards the undoing of repression—in this case, the drive towards the restoration of attachment. It is here suggested that it is precisely this reparative urge that is involved in the homosexual impulse, that is, that this impulse is essentially motivated by the need to make good earlier deficits in the parent-child relationship. The persisting need for love from the same sex stems from, and is to be correlated with, the earlier unmet need for love from the parent of the same sex, or rather, the inability to receive such love, whether or not it was offered.[6]

Homosexuality can thus be described as a reparative urge, a desperate effort to have needs met. The person suffering from the homosexual condition is thus caught in an ambivalent situation. He or she has defensively detached from the parent of the same sex in order to avoid further hurt, while at the same time trying to become attached to members of the same sex in order to have basic needs met.

One young man said, "All I want are male friends who can show me love and friendship without running away all the time." The tragedy of his situation was that he and his chosen companions settled for sex and did not offer to meet the basic needs which they all had. The anonymous sex which many homosexuals experience seems only to strengthen the reparative urge and leave the person more desperate.

Stan said, "Until I stopped cruising and began to look at my needs instead of having them blindly met I was caught with no place to go. The habit got stronger and the needs got greater with no resolution."

God intended that basic needs be met through the parent-child relationship. The problem is that the child perceives that the parent either cannot or will not meet those needs. Thus, when the child detaches from the parent, the needs have been abnormally left unmet; as the child develops, he or she will seek to have those needs met by persons of the same sex. This is what Moberly calls the reparative drive.

The need of a person for same-sex love is not abnormal; it is a normal one, which has been distorted by the defensive detachment which has occurred from the same-sex parent. Thus, the lesbian seeking a mother figure may be an accurate picture; but the need for such a relationship should be seen as normal, not abnormal. It is the eroticization of the need for mother love which introduces the abnormality.

The fact that homo-emotional needs are often, though by no means always, eroticized, has tended to distract attention from the significance of the homosexual condition in itself. It is not surprising that someone who has attained physiological maturity should interpret his or her deepest emotional needs as sexual, but this is to mistake the essential character of these needs. Sexual expression is not appropriate to the normal parent-child relationship. Nor, as a corollary, is it appropriate to any relationship which, however adult in other respects, is significantly determined by the attempt to meet non-adult attachment needs. In the homosexual condition psychological needs that are essentially pre-adult remain in a person who is in other respects adult. Homosexual activity implies the eroticization of deficits in growth that remain outstanding, and this is, fundamentally, a confusion of the emotional needs of the non-adult with the physiological desires of the adult. Sexuality is intended to express the desires both of physiological maturity and of psychological maturity, in co-ordination with each other. The one should not be isolated from the other. Where there is a lack of such co-ordination, deficits in growth should be fulfilled non-sexually, and in this way an integrated basis for a sexually expressed relationship will be attained.[7]

Counselors often become confused as they observe that many of their homosexual counselees apparently have warm, loving relationships with members of the opposite sex which would be the envy of many married heterosexuals. What is the problem? Why doesn't the closeness and intimacy convert to sexual energy as it does in many relationships? One person said, "Just when I find someone I can really love and who really loves, me, I find out he is gay."

The point is that opposite-sex relationships are not relevant to the meeting of needs which stem from deficits with the same-sex parent. Opposite-sex relationships have value for their own sake, but when proposed as a solution for the homosexual condition they will only leave the counselee feeling confused and misunderstood.

This conclusion points out why, if Moberly's theory is right, much counseling that has focused upon building relationships and even heightening sexual attraction for the opposite sex has failed. It didn't address the problem. Once the true problem has been addressed and the needs of the counselee have been met in a noneroticized way, then the possibility of opposite sex relations can be addressed. Reversing this order will not work.

I have discovered that the homosexual condition in a very high percentage of the counselees with whom I work can be explained by Moberly's theory. I do not believe it explains all homosexual causality or behavior. But it is a very relevant theory with which the counselor needs to be thoroughly familiar, and which needs to be understood not only by counselors, but by pastors, friends, and others who wish to help. It has direct implications for the church in attempting to be relevant to the homosexual community without succumbing to the "God made us this way" view. I cannot think of a better setting than the church to provide a place where the need for love, identification, and belonging can be met in a noneroticized fashion.

The question is, do we have the courage to offer such intense relationships to such needy people? Do we as friends and counselors have the courage to love? One prominent Christian therapist has stated that he has not had a male homosexual with whom he has worked "fall in love" with him without becoming free of his homosexual struggle. It takes courage to trust your own values and self-control in order to offer a loving relationship which is not eroticized. I believe that this is precisely the kind of relationship Jesus had with his friends of both sexes—love without eroticism.

SOCIAL LEARNING THEORY

The social learning theory was postulated by Neal Miller in the 1950s and later popularized by Albert Bandura and his colleagues at Stanford University in the 1960s. The theory emphasizes imitation and observation learning. Its relevance to sexual behavior has been discussed by Hamachek:

As you might suspect, parents are enormously important in determining a child's sex-role preference. Probably the most fortunate pre-schooler is the one who has so adequate a father (male model) and mother (female model) that he comes early to prefer the sex-role dictated by his physiology, moves along naturally and easily with its development, and eventually identifies thoroughly with it. There seems little question that the basic components of sex-typing are undoubtedly acquired at home, largely through imitation of, and identification with, the parent of the same sex.[8]

This theory has been useful in explaining a variety of human behavior forms, such as aggression, social roles, fears, and even some forms of mental illness. Embedded in the theory are several key concepts which I believe are very helpful in explaining how various aspects of homosexuality may be acquired. These concepts are: observational learning, social reinforcement, and cognitive set, which I have described in my interpretation of the theory as "filtering."

This section, in fact this chapter, presents an expansion and a rethinking of my views on causality which appear in chapter 7 of my book, *Sexual Sanity*.[9] The reader will also note that chapter 8, on the assessment interviews, is designed to help the counselor gather data which is particularly relevant to the Moberly point of view and the social learning approach.

Observational Learning

The social learning approach affirms the importance of observation and imitation in learning many types of behavior. It suggests that people do not have to have direct experience to learn specific responses. How might this apply to the acquisition of the homosexual condition?

Young children engage in two important types of observation which may have a bearing on their sexual-response patterns. They observe the sexual behavior of parents and other significant adults with whom they may identify and they observe as well as participate in sexual behavior amongst their peers. These opportunities to observe begin in early childhood and may affect the person's sexual preference even prior to the onset of puberty. Brian is a good example.

Brian's early observation about sex was that a man cannot give pleasure to or receive pleasure from a woman. He had two main recollections of his parents' relationship: their fighting and the grim looks on their faces when his mother would push his father away. These memories were building blocks for his own experience.

Brian's sexual experience began at age thirteen. He remembers trying to make love to a neighbor girl in an abandoned house. She was stronger than he and pushed him away. He remembers feeling totally defeated. He wondered about his masculinity at that point, but didn't give it much thought.

When Brian entered high school, however, he became aware that he was sexually aroused by males, especially in his physical education classes. An only child, he was not used to nudity and loose sexual talk. When he occasionally found himself aroused, he didn't know what to think about it. So he responded by withdrawing as much as possible.

Brian's observations that contact with the opposite sex was not only dissatisfying but aversive set the stage for his personal adolescent sexual experience to be interpreted in a particular way. He did not believe that contact with girls could be rewarding so he ignored them. This was not to say that the concept of sexual pleasure was foreign to him—he had started masturbating with his friends at an early age.

Although the effects of masturbation upon the development of homosexuality are unclear, it may be a significant factor for some people. Tripp observes:

> Certainly most adolescent homosexual activities are inconsequential. The masturbatory sessions of groups of boys (to see who can reach orgasm first or ejaculate farthest) as well as most one-to-one contacts amount to hardly more than explorations in erotica. Even homosexual males describe these kinds of experiences as having been impersonal and unimportant. Of the remaining much smaller number of instances in which early homosexual experiences do lead to ongoing patterns, a few qualify as a kind of simple, direct conditioning; others are not so simple.
>
> There are adolescents (and a few late-arriving adults) who begin having homosexual experiences which at first may have little appeal and only gradually become meaningful.[10]

Exploration with erotica may not be as innocent as Tripp implies.

What observational learning or conditioning takes place here? First, there is the association of sexual pleasure (orgasm through masturbation) with male faces and male companions. Females are not usually present in these group experiences, thus the opportunity for association of pleasure with females is not available. Second, there is the opportunity for young men to observe males pleasuring each other as mutual masturbation often takes place. Even if the person is too shy to participate, the conditioning will take place. Thirdly, there is the observation that sex is pleasurable but must be kept highly secret because it is bad. I believe this is preparatory learning for the anonymous, pleasure-seeking type of sex life that many homosexuals live. The fear of getting caught just serves to heighten the level of sexual arousal and further convince the person of his or her homosexual orientation.[11]

Young children may also learn through observation that sex between a man and a woman is nasty and should never be engaged in. Sometimes the prohibition is given in such a blanket way that it doesn't even allow for sexual activity in marriage. One of my counselees reports how he came to believe that sex with women is prohibited. His father, upon catching him masturbating while looking at a picture of a man and woman having intercourse, told him, "That is bad and I don't ever want to hear of you doing it. If I ever see you hard again I will cut that thing off." Needless to say, this experience left my counselee in a real state of turmoil from that time forward. He told me, "I was scared to death—I didn't have any basis not to believe him. He was a mean, harsh man."

Some of the scare tactics which Christians often use may lead to the learning of fears and prohibitions which set the stage for one's later learning of a homosexual response and lifestyle. Back to the story of Brian.

When Brian was seventeen he had his first homosexual encounter. He performed fellatio for a neighbor man. Even though the process made him physically ill, his strongest memory is of the man smiling and writhing in pleasure. This memory stands in sharp contrast to what he saw in his parents' relationship and what he experienced at age thirteen with the neighbor girl.

Brian became more curious about the same sex after this encounter, and the next time he was propositioned by a male he accepted. This time he didn't vomit, and he both gave and received pleasure. This experience confirmed his early perception of himself as a homosexual and his belief about himself affected how he viewed his world. Each new homosexual encounter strengthened his perception, and Brian began to develop an identity as a homosexual.

Because Brian was a believer he chose not to continue practicing homosexuality, but his life was very difficult. During his college days he tried to go straight. He dated a few girls and even became engaged. He did not try to make love or engage in any form of sexual activity with his fiancée, eventually breaking off the engagement because of fear of not being able to satisfy her sexually.

A few years later he began to practice homosexuality on a regular basis. He truly believed his only other option was to remain sexually dormant, an option he chose not to exercise. After being in therapy a while, he began to relearn his sexual identity and reorient himself to the opposite sex. His same-sex sexual differentiation, although strong, was not permanent.

Brian's case is not sufficient to prove that same-sex preference is learned. It merely illustrates that same-sex preference can be explained from a learning point of view and that sexual preference can sometimes be relearned. We need to be careful in drawing any all-inclusive conclusions about sexual preference. I do not agree with the contention of the gay rights movement that homosexuals are born that way and therefore cannot change. An individual who accepts this position may be selling his birthright to natural heterosexual experience.

Social Reinforcement

This concept would suggest that the pattern of sexual response acquired by the person will be the pattern which is reinforced by the environment. It begins with observational learning but goes beyond that to the actual experience of the person and the response of his or her environment to that experience.

Margaret said, "I grew up relating sexually to women—that was all I knew. We hugged, kissed, slept together, and at an early age began to touch each other for pleasure. I never thought of myself as a homosexual because I still had the 'little girl dream' of marriage and a family. The dream, however, was left in shambles when I began to relate to guys and it was *not fun*. I wanted to stay away from the pain men had caused me and get back to the pleasure I had felt with my friends."

Social reinforcement suggests that people will learn the sexual behaviors and thus the sexual orientation which they find positively reinforced. On the other hand, sexual activity which is aversive will be suppressed. People do the things from which they get pleasure and they avoid hurtful activities. On this basis, I contend that many women become lesbians because they have found that women are better lovers. They take more time to provide pleasure and they (usually) avoid hurting.

In trying to explain his sexual behavior to me, one counselee said, "I grew up in the city where you would do whatever you could find to do to 'get your rocks off' (street language for orgasm or ejaculation). We didn't care what we did as long as it made us feel good. This has resulted in a lot of confusion for me. I'm just as homosexual as I am heterosexual. The only difference is that it is easier to get pleasure homosexually. Men I meet on the street want what I want and they don't ask any questions."

The reinforcement principle suggests that behavior which is followed by a positive or pleasurable consequence will increase in frequency. This reinforcement can be of three basic kinds: vicarious—seeing others receive pleasure sexually; social—having others approve of your sexual behavior toward them; or personal—experiencing pleasure from your own sexual activity. Each is important to an understanding of how homosexual behavior may get started.

I have worked with some individuals who were deeply involved (even to the point of being arrested) in homosexual activity even though they claimed that their sexual leanings were toward the opposite sex, not the same sex. In assessing the situation with these men, I discovered three important variables.

1. They had all received strong injunctions against sexual activity with women. First Corinthians 7:1 had been quoted repeatedly.

2. They had also redefined physical activity with men as nonsexual because it obviously couldn't lead to intercourse. This is a distorted kind of legalism which defines away sin by employing technicalities.

3. They were all pleasure seekers who were addicted sexually by the pleasure they were receiving. Their homosexual behavior was sustained by the outward pleasure received, not by some kind of inner drive. I believe that many homosexuals fall into the category of sexual addicts, although the fear of AIDS has cut the numbers and the amount of sexual activity of the homosexual, as well as those of the heterosexual pleasure seekers.

Filtering

The concept of filtering or forming a "cognitive set" is closely related to what is called "learning set" or a "cognitive map." It is a rule by which a person interprets learning tasks or stimuli from the environment.

The following diagram by Judson Swihart illustrates how the filtering process affects communication. The key idea is that certain incoming messages are not heard and are thus filtered out, just as a camera filter takes out certain rays of the sun or a coffee filter takes out grounds or impurities. The diagram[12] also points out that the filtering process also affects what we tell ourselves about outside stimuli and also what we actually feel about our perceptions of the stimuli. As you can see, a lot of things happen between the incoming message and the response. Our behavior is never as spontaneous as it appears to be. This is true of sexual behavior as well as communication.

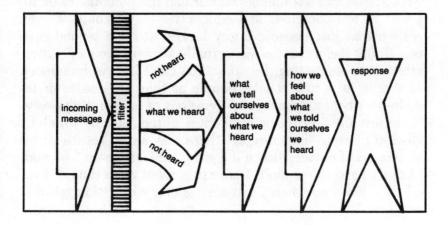

Look now at how the filtering process may affect the learning of homosexual behavior. We will continue with the illustration of Brian. Earlier, I stated that "each new homosexual encounter strengthened his filtering system, and Brian began to develop an identity as a homosexual." What does this mean? Put simply, it means as persons have experience with homosexuality, they will reach a place where they accept the label "homosexual" or "lesbian," and from that time forward will interpret all the things that happen to them from that perspective. This results in two unfortunate things which affect the acceptance of homosexual lifestyle.

First, stimuli which would suggest heterosexual tendencies are denied or filtered out. The brain tries to clear up ambivalence so the heterosexual input is filtered out as irrelevant. I find that many of my counselees have blanked out their memory of periods of heterosexual activity because it does not fit with their newly acquired belief that they are gay—and gays have not and never will be attracted to the opposite sex—so the experience cannot be considered. They are often shocked when they are helped through counseling to remember more clearly these experiences which have been filtered out.

The second unfortunate thing which happens is that most of the same-sex contact seems to get filtered in. The process goes something like this. "I am a homosexual, so men must be attracted to me." Stan said, "I believed that every contact with a male was a sexual contact or had the potential to be so. I was so self-conscious and egocentric that I couldn't even realize that just because a guy looked at me a second time that didn't mean that he was sexually attracted to me." Later, after some counseling, he said, "You can't believe how much of a relief it is to just take people as they are—male or female—without all the mental gyrations of interpreting everything sexually." With the weakening of the filter by which he labeled himself "homosexual" there was also a return of his awareness of choice. "Even if a gay guy sizes me up," he said, "I don't have to respond. I am not a robot even though I really felt like one when I was seeing everything through that mind set."

BIOCHEMICAL CONTRIBUTIONS TO HOMOSEXUALITY

The study of possible biological or chemical contributions to behaviors, including homosexuality, is called psychoneuroendocrinology. In this field the work of Dr. John Money and his associates at Johns Hopkins University is the standard by which all other works are to be judged. In a 1987 review of his work entitled "Sin, Sickness, or Status? Homosexual Gender Identity and Psychoneuroendocrinology" he concluded,

As in subhuman primates, in the human species sexuoerotic status is dependent not only on prenatal hormonalization, but also on postnatal socialization effects. There are several different human hermaphroditic syndromes each of which makes its own specific contribution to the science of homosexuology and to the understanding of genetic, prenatal-hormonal, pubertal-hormonal, and socialization determinants of being gay, straight, or bisexual. In combination, they indicate that sexual orientation is not under the direct governance of chromosomes and genes, and that, whereas it is not foreordained by prenatal brain hormonalization it is influenced thereby, and is also strongly dependent on postnatal socialization.[13]

Money's work basically leaves open the possibility that persons who experienced hormonal imbalance before birth may have become predisposed to the homosexual condition. The frequency of such predisposition is unclear. As stated earlier, I do not believe that all persons who practice homosexuality have been biochemically predisposed. I believe that the majority of those who practice homosexuality do so because of social learning factors or factors related to parent-child relations as described by Moberly. Money's work and the work of Günter Dörner cited earlier are worthy of careful consideration. They present several facts which must be carefully considered.

First, homosexual behavior can be created in the laboratory by the alteration of biochemical conditions. This cannot be denied. It leaves open the possibility of the homosexual condition being at least partially set prior to birth. Two biological conditions have been demonstrated: prenatal maternal stress, that is, stress during pregnancy, has been shown to have a demasculinizing effect on the babies born, at least in rats. It has also been shown that the ingestion of barbiturates by the pregnant female will have a demasculinizing effect on the unborn male rat pups and that when the hormonal makeup of unborn rats contains a high level of androgens the effect will be to masculinize the unborn female rat pups. Thus, too high a testosterone level in utero may contribute to lesbianism in females while too low a testosterone level may contribute to homosexuality in males.

How this happens becomes more clear when you consider the "Adam/Eve Principle" of prenatal hormonalization as described by Money.

In gender transposition, the phylogenetic basis of the transposition and its attachment to sex and eroticism is epitomized in the Adam/Eve Principle, namely, nature's rudimentary principle of sexual differentiation, which is to differentiate a female and to have to add something to differentiate a male. In gender transposition, the successive phases of differentiation, beginning prenatally and continuing postnatally, do not proceed concordantly in the usual orderly fashion. Discordance may begin prenatally under hormonal influence so that, at birth, a baby is at risk postnatally for a transposed gender status, provided convergent social influences and experiences increase the risk. . . .

According to the Adam/Eve Principle, simply stated, if the fetal brain is not hormonalized, it will develop from its early, sexually bipotential stage to be, like Eve, feminine. To be like Adam, it must be hormonalized. The hormone is testosterone or one of its derivative metabolites.[14]

The Adam/Eve Principle makes it easier to understand how male children might be more predisposed to homosexuality than female children just because males have to add something while females are already headed toward becoming

"Eve." Obviously, much research is to be done if we are to understand this puzzle. Masculinization does not equal lesbianism. Demasculinization does not equal homosexuality. Many effeminate men function as exclusively heterosexual while many masculine-appearing women are very content being wives and mothers.

Although one is tempted to want to discredit these data because the experiments were conducted on rats and not humans, the results are in line with some of the conclusions drawn by Dörner who traced down the histories of many homosexuals and found the mothers to be under unusual stress during pregnancy. *Stress undoubtedly affects hormonal conditions and hormonal conditions in utero affect the sexual predispositions of the unborn.* There are no clear links which support people's claims that they were born homosexual. On the other hand, we must understand that the same sexual differentiation in the brain which takes place prior to birth in rodents also appears to take place in humans. All of the mechanisms are not clearly understood; in fact, the areas of the brain of different species in which sexual differentiation takes place is not even clear. Thus, Louis Goren of Voriji Universiteit in Holland states, "I do not believe that the hypothalamus is sex-differentiated in the human brain. It is in the rat, for sure. That is why Dörner is right when he talks about rats but wrong when he talks about humans."[15]

For the scientist as well as the layman the various studies and arguments regarding the possible biochemical causes of homosexuality are incomplete and confusing. They do, however, demand a hearing. We need to continue to evaluate these findings and try honestly to interpret them to our homosexual counselees. The myths we can dispel, such as the belief that if one's father is homosexual the child will be also. It is not passed along like blue eyes or curly hair. We can also dispel the myth that homosexuality is controlled by current hormone levels. It is not. I believe that John Money has given as concise a statement as can be made at this time. He writes,

With respect to orientation as homosexual or bisexual, there is no human evidence that prenatal hormonalization

71

alone, independently of postnatal history, inexorably pre-
ordains either orientation. Rather, neonatal antecedents
may facilitate a homosexual or bisexual orientation, provided the postnatal determinants in the social and commu-
nicational history are also facilitative.[16]

In another place, Money concluded:

After conception and before the sex organs develop, everyone is bisexual because everyone has the embryonic
beginnings of both types of sex organ. By the time of
birth, however, differentiation of the genitals has usually
occurred. This differentiation is taken to indicate the sex
of the baby, but scientifically, there is still no way of as-
certaining how sexuality is governed in the brain. It is
highly probable, however, that sex-related pathways in
the brain are programed to make it either easy or difficult to conform to one or the other of the strict gender
stereotypes.[17]

CONCLUSIONS

What can we say? What do we know about the causes of
homosexuality? Are there conclusions which can be drawn?

First, there is a growing body of research which supports
the idea that sex differentiation is predisposed before the child
is born. This is not to say that it is *determined* prior to birth. It
only means that there are leanings toward a sexual preference
which set the stage for postnatal influences to further establish
a preference.

Second, the degree to which prenatal dispositions can be
altered is hotly debated. Money feels they are very resistant
to change once they have been confirmed by postnatal experience.

Third, there is evidence to support other causes of homosexuality. Both the work of Elizabeth Moberly regarding the effects of parent-child relations and the social learning theory
seem highly relevant. Both of these positions would argue that
change in the homosexual condition is possible. If behavior is

learned or results from a reaction to social conditions it seems reasonable to believe that it can be reversed.

Finally, if, as the author contends, a high percentage of cases of homosexuality are best explained by social learning or parent-child explanations, then it would follow that there is much work for the counselor to do. People can change and we can help them to change. There is hope, and as counselors we must continue to work and learn so that we can bring hope to those we serve.

CHAPTER FIVE

LESBIANISM AND SEXUAL CONFUSION

THE ISSUES RELATED TO FEMALE HOMOSEXUALITY, called lesbianism, are sometimes even more difficult to understand than those related to male homosexuality. The word *lesbian* means "of the people of Lesbos," an island in the Aegean Sea. The island was known for the practice of homosexuality by Sappho and her followers.[1]

It is interesting that lesbianism designates a distinct form of the practice of homosexuality by women, while there is no special name for the practice of male homosexuality. Indeed, it seems appropriate because in my judgment and the judgment of others, there are some very real differences.

Women have a different arousal system than men. The

masculine arousal tends to be very visual and genital. The response of women, on the other hand, is more tied to affection and seems to involve more of the total body. Because the signs of sexual arousal in the woman are less obvious than in the man, women can often reinterpret sexual excitement or channel it into other activities if the time and/or place of arousal is inappropriate for sexual expression.

Women also work on a different cueing system than men. The sexual cues that women give to other women are more subtle than those given to men. Women rely on eye contact, intensified attention, and other types of close, interpersonal connections in order to show sexual interest. In short, they lead with their persons not with their bodies as men do. A woman may be afraid to believe that another woman is sexually interested in her, but as time goes by and the affectionate interpersonal contact continues, sexual activity may begin.

LESBIAN BACKGROUNDS

My counseling experience has shown that in contrast to male homosexuals, many lesbians have had heterosexual experience. A typical pattern is for the woman to have had an unsuccessful marriage, an oppressive experience with men, or a series of unsatisfying sexual relationships with men which have left her vulnerable to sexual involvement with someone of the same sex. In fact, most lesbians are more apt to be bisexual than their male counterparts.

Women, however, long for affection and more equal relationships which may lead them to same-sex involvement. If they are not treated rightly by men, they may react by turning their sexual attention to persons of the same sex. Many lesbians have been sexually abused either before or during marriage or both. Payne writes of one such woman,

Lana's story is typical of this condition found in lesbian behavior. Besides the absence of mother-love and fondling, she was from a very early age sexually abused by her father's younger brother. As an adult, she had conflicting feelings about this sexual abuse because her need for touch was to some extent gratified in these sordid and degrading circumstances. She was at once ashamed of how her youthful uncle had treated her, and guilty for needing the touch, however perverse and unloving. These circumstances were enough to start her on the road to thinking of herself as primarily a sexual being and of receiving and giving love mostly in sensual terms. It should be emphasized that it does not take circumstances as extreme as incest to effect this in a woman; sometimes merely having parents whose problems revolve around sexual tensions can make this dimension of one's person seem to be the prime one.[2]

A much smaller group of women have not been sexually involved with men and have at times been attracted to both men and women. Involvement with the same sex usually begins because of loneliness and there usually isn't an initial intention of the relationships becoming sexual. It usually begins with a desire for closeness and affection which then turns to sexual gratification or at least exploration. Masters and Johnson cite one such case.

I had been dating a guy I was very friendly with for about a year with a good sexual relationship. Then I suddenly found myself making it with my roommate, who slowly but expertly introduced me to how two women can make love. I really enjoyed both kinds of sex and both personal relationships, so I continued them for some while until my graduate school career was over and I moved to a new town.[3]

CAUSAL FACTORS

Discussion regarding causes of lesbianism tends to focus much less on biochemical or genetic issues as compared to male homosexuality. The disputed evidence for physical causes of male homosexuality is even weaker when it comes to lesbianism. Money and Wiedeking write:

Sexologists agree that the incidence of gender identity/role disorders is greater in males than in females, though there are as yet no fixed statistics. The embryology of prenatal hormonal regulation of sex differentiation clearly shows that nature's first choice is to differentiate the morphology of a female. The differentiation of male morphology requires that something be added (the "Adam principle"). This something is, for the most part, androgen released by the fetal testes.[4]

Social Learning

The majority of the evidence would suggest that lesbianism is learned in the social context of loving relationships with persons of the same sex. Female friendships provide opportunity for affection to be demonstrated and for caring to be shown. These needs are basic to all human beings. Lesbianism occurs when the needs are eroticized. This means that the expression of love and caring takes on a sexual component. This sexual component stands in sharp contrast to the kind of lovemaking that most women who choose lesbianism have experienced with male lovers. Masters and Johnson write:

> The homosexual couples tended to move slowly through excitement and to linger at plateau stages of stimulative response, making each step in tension increment something to be appreciated. Stimulative approaches were usually free-flowing rather than forceful or directive in character, and rarely was there overt evidence of goal orientation. The exchange of pleasure at all levels of sexual excitation appeared to be of greatest importance, with the orgasmic experience merely one more step in the pleasure sequence.
>
> In contrast, the sexual behavior of the married couples was far more performance-oriented. An apparent pressure to "get the job done" was usually evident during partner manipulation and fellatio/cunnilingus and was consistently present during coition.[5]

Because women are often very attentive to each other it is natural that the women who experience a tenderness and caring in same-sex relationships would be inclined to continue in that type of lovemaking. Many continue bisexually for a time and then decide to avoid men sexually altogether.

A thirty-year-old woman writes of her lesbian relationship as compared to her experiences with men,

> You just can't compare the quality of sex with someone you hardly know and feel nothing for with the quality of sex in a caring relationship. Casual sex is just mechanical, one-dimensional release. Sex with someone I care about is warmer and psychologically far more satisfying.[6]

Within the Christian context where even heterosexual sex is discouraged until after marriage, young women often become sexually confused. They may successfully avoid contacts with men which result in sexual arousal only to find themselves highly aroused after a moment of tenderness with a roommate at a Christian college.

One young woman said, "I have never been attracted to females, but I have a very high need for affection. I was afraid to let my boyfriend meet that need for fear I would lose sexual control. Everything was fine until a couple months ago. My roommate and I were lying on her bed looking at some photos. When we got through them she put her head on my stomach and we just stayed there talking for a long time. I didn't think anything about it. I just felt warm inside. Later that week we started pillow-fighting on my bed and somehow we ended up in each other's arms. It scared both of us a little but we didn't really talk about it. The next night, however, things were different. It was like we both knew we were about to do something we knew we shouldn't, but we did it anyway. We lay on the bed and kissed and touched each other's breasts and thighs. I tried to tell myself it was okay, but I realized that it was sexual. I was aroused and didn't know how to handle it. We told each other we had to stop and we did for a week and then we slipped again. I don't think I'm a lesbian but I'm really confused and upset with myself."

In this short statement by my counselee you can trace the social reinforcers which led to the lesbian interaction. Initially there was the warm friendship as the friends lay together on the bed sharing the photos. This was followed by the physical closeness and the reinforcing conversation. Next came play, the expression of the child which drew them closer together and resulted in holding each other. Each of these steps was reinforcing and eventually they engaged in presexual and sexual behavior.

In situations where the counselee has had negative experiences with males, the tender caring she experiences in the same-sex relationship may be an even more powerful rein• forcer. Janet was attracted to males but had been abused or treated disrespectfully in almost every heterosexual relationship she had been a part of. After a lesbian encounter she said, "I know it sounds awful, but it just felt so good to have someone care about what I wanted for a change." When sexual experience is associated with strong social reinforcers like caring and tenderness such reinforcers tend to strengthen the appeal of the sexual, even in situations where previously there may not have been attraction to the same sex.

The assessment interviews can enable the counselor and the counselee to trace the social learning of the behavior and then help them make decisions about avoiding situations which strengthen the pattern. Learned behavior is weakened by nonpractice. When this is the case the person may be ready to learn new, positive behaviors toward the opposite sex.

Disruptions in Relationship with the Same-Sex Parent

Traditional psychoanalytic literature pointed to the breakdown in the relationship with the opposite-sex parent as a possible causal factor in homosexuality. Recent work by Elizabeth Moberly, as we have already noted, has suggested, however, that the key relationship in the movement toward lesbianism is the relationship with the mother.

It is normal for women who have defensively detached from their mothers to search for a mother figure to whom they can now attach. The attachment is not the problem; it is a solution to the underlying problem, particularly if the contact is not sexualized.

The issues of defensive detachment and the critical role that unfulfilled needs play in the development of the homosexual condition have been discussed in chapter 4. As we have seen, relationships with the same-sex parent do not have to be abusive or horrible. There is no objective standard for evaluating what quality of relationship is substandard. The key issue is how the young woman perceives the situation with the mother. If she perceives the mother to be incapable of meeting her needs she may choose to seek such fulfillment in a relationship with another woman. If this occurs it is possible that the attempts to have those needs met may be eroticized and lesbianism will develop.

The fantasies of many lesbians are often more affection-oriented than erotic. Judy longed for her female friend to hold her and kiss her cheeks. Nancy wanted to be held on her mother's lap and have her stroke her hair. Betty thought her fantasies were strictly erotic until she began to consider them more fully. She longed to kiss her friend's nipples and play like she was nursing. One day in a wide-eyed moment of insight she said, "I think I want to be a baby again. She is my mom and I want to be a baby again to see if she will love me this time." This insight served to release Betty from excessive guilt and she was more open to seeing herself as having the potential to choose the kind of sexual lifestyle she would follow.

When a woman labels herself as lesbian she will label all her experiences so they fit into that pattern. If she sees herself as confused or trying to work through unmet needs she will label her experiences from that perspective. I am convinced that it is not an accident that many young women choose, or are chosen by, lovers who are old enough to be their mothers or play that role in their lives. They are looking for unmet needs to be met and those needs just happen to get tied into the erotic experiences. Discussing lesbianism, Barnhouse writes,

The psychological basis for most lesbianism lies more in the other two areas: unresolved issues around dependency upon the mother and fear of heterosexuality. Some readers will be old enough to remember the proverb, "A son is a son 'til he gets him a wife, a daughter's a daughter all of her life."

The family behavior patterns which have been found in the background of lesbians are exaggerations of these difficulties. Some women have serious, unsatisfied dependency needs because they received inadequate mothering during infancy and childhood. The homosexual adaptation in such cases is essentially a regressive attempt to secure the safety and pleasure of identification with the maternal principle. When there are several daughters in a family, only one of whom was rejected or inadequately mothered and later became a lesbian, investigation usually reveals that at this particular birth a son was urgently desired, or that for other reasons the child did not conform to the pattern of temperament and behavior which her mother thought suitable or desirable in girls. Because of this, she grew up with a lonely sense of exclusion from the intimate feminine world shared by her mother and sisters and her eventual lesbianism is an attempt to make up for this loss.[7]

The fear of heterosexuality which Barnhouse refers to would be a social-learning cause of lesbianism. This observation supports my belief that there are multiple causal factors at work.

Barnhouse has suggested one other disorder in the relationship with the same-sex parent which contributes to lesbianism. This is the problem of prolonged intimacy or what others call enmeshed relationships.

Women who have never adequately relinquished their infantile attachment to their mothers find it more difficult to take the subsequent steps in psychosexual development which are required for the establishment of a satisfactory heterosexual adjustment. This is particularly true since some degree of abnormal fathering can also always be demonstrated.[8]

In discussing enmeshed relationships, Dr. Dorthea McArthur has observed that the mother may convey to the child a number of directives or "commandments." At least three of these may affect the development of the homosexual condition. The commandments are:

You will not be a whole, separate person, but remain a perfect part of myself.

As a part of me, you must not dare to love anyone but me. . . . not even your father. You will not have any emotional or physical need for anyone but me. I will provide all.

You will not leave me physically or emotionally. If you do, I will withdraw from you. If circumstances part us, you will be in a continuous state of anxious alertness to intuit my psychological needs. You will conduct yourself in ways which validate and calm me. Any failure in this task will bring a terrible emptiness, anxiety and guilt.[9]

These two aspects of the breakdown in the mother-daughter relationship suggest a delicate balance in parenting. Too little love and concern may result in the defensive detachment of which Moberly writes. Over control and failure to let the daughter develop her own life may result in a lifelong attachment to mother and/or a mother figure, which may also be eroticized.

Biological Variations

Although biochemical theories regarding lesbianism are tentative and not well-researched, current explanations tend to focus on masculinization of the female child in utero. Dörner states his belief:

When a female embryo is exposed to a high level of testosterone, the brain becomes masculinized and the girl becomes lesbian.[10]

Although this point of view is appealing because it parallels the thinking regarding male homosexuality, both the evidence and the research are weak. It seems highly probable that many girls, whose sexual differentiation is such that they develop male interests during adolescence, will experience sexual confusion and will later develop lesbian or bisexual tendencies. Such tendencies are learned in accordance with the social-learning model discussed earlier.

One client said, "I had nowhere to go. My interests were more like boys and there wasn't much of an emphasis upon sports for women at that time. The boys pulled away from me and my mom wasn't real pleased with me. I got caught in the rut of trying to please father through sports and trying to deny what femininity I felt."

Women who choose to masculinize themselves by talk, wardrobe, or actions may do so because they are trying to fit in. Our society does not allow for much variation of physique or behavior. It is highly likely that those who experience variation from social norms may feel they have no choice but to move toward lesbianism if their needs for acceptance and affection are to be met. It is a very complex issue.

PERTINENT COUNSELING ISSUES

As you approach counseling with lesbian counselees you need to be particularly aware of your own biases or stereotypes. If you are a male counselor your own sexuality may be challenged or you may think that your counselee has a bias against or a hatred for you because you are male. Such views could destroy the counseling relationship. If you are female you may fear your counselee because you do not understand her. If she is different from you, you may withdraw at first. The only solution is time and understanding. Look for the person—don't get lost in a stereotype.

If your counselee does fit a stereotype do not allow your view to stop there. Continue to explore the value of the person and to allow her to explore who she wants to become. Some lesbian counselees struggle, wondering if they are or can become feminine. Your support with them during this process can be invaluable. When counselees are involved in this process they need female guidance and support. They need to define themselves as females, and not females for men. Male input may be helpful, but work with a same-sex counselor or at least the support of a same-sex friend, along with the counselor, is very important. As a male counselor I do not hesitate to affirm the attractiveness and femininity of my lesbian counselees, but I want them to feel good about their total womanhood, not just their attractiveness. I also recognize I don't know much about women and cannot assume that I am able to guide a woman toward her views of being feminine.

Dependency and Control

Another key issue in working with lesbian counselees is the issue of dependency. Some lesbians become highly dependent upon their partners or lovers while others become dominant or over-controlling. The point for the counselor is that the issue needs to be explored. Whether your counselee is dominant or submissive she needs to understand her feelings or attitudes. Exploring this area may lead to a profitable awareness of attitudes toward both father and mother. Counselees may not like who they are but may not know how to change.

Jackie said, "I always pick female friends who dominate me. I don't know why, because I swore that wouldn't happen. My mother always ran over me and I hated it. I just can't seem to find another type of person." During counseling Jackie realized that each time she started into a relationship where she was dominated she told herself things would be different. She was expecting to be loved and respected, not dominated, but each "new mother" turned out the same. Following this discovery the doors were open for Jackie to learn how to evaluate people better and also how to say no to potentially nonproductive situations even though the temptation to believe that the new relationship would be different remained.

It is important for counselees to know that they may choose partners who meet a need—but that that need may not be healthy. Beverly became involved with a woman who tried to control her totally. She needed to learn to take charge of her own life. Connie, on the other hand, was usually the dominant person in her relationships. She said, "The hardest thing I had to learn was that people would still love me even if I wasn't making them do so." As she learned to control her dominance she actually felt more loved, even though it was uncomfortable. "I have found that people accepted me for who I was rather than because I was forcing them to do what I wanted. It is really nice," she said.

When people become able to relate and develop confidence

in themselves the importance of dependence or dominance lessens.

Issues of control often come up in counseling with lesbians because many times they are struggling with being controlled by one or more of their parents. Marlene said, "My mother never let me control anything. She even told me when to go to bed after I was in college. Now I'm mixed up. I feel like I want to control others, but I don't even have confidence that I can control myself."

I teach counselees to learn to *state* their needs to people rather than demand that those needs be met or believe that no one would want to meet their needs. I call it learning to relate person to person. We each share what we think and feel and need; we each respond to the other as best we can. Relationships are not perfect, but they become healthy as we feel less controlled and less controlling. We can be real people striving to be sensitive to each other's needs.

People who are over-controlling usually hate themselves and have little respect for the weak people they control. People who are controlled, on the other hand, usually devalue themselves but secretly hate the people who are controlling them. It is a vicious circle, but one that needs to be broken. Understanding some of these psychologically confusing areas paves the way for working through the sexual confusion which lesbians experience.

Effects of Conditional Love

Most lesbians have been victimized by conditional love. They have experienced "I'll love you when" from their parents, and have been treated as sex objects by the men with whom they have been involved. These experiences have resulted in alienation from parents and a disdain for the opposite sex. Attempts to find love have often been disastrous and the love deficit has grown even larger. Camille reported, "I could never please my mother and I always felt that whatever I did I would fall just short of her really loving me. She would slip me a carrot once in a while but when I would reach for it, it would be gone. She didn't seem to care that I was her daughter—she only blackmailed me. If I would *do* more, then she might love me."

Unfortunately, the searching-for-love game Camille learned to play with her mother was the same game she felt compelled to play with the men in her life. She was constantly being told that if she would change in certain ways, she would be loved. One of her first boyfriends said, "You would be a really neat person if you would just lose some weight." She hadn't dated very long until she heard, "I'm not going to spend money on you unless I get something in return." After she had sex with the guy he left her for a new conquest. Camille cried, "I was devastated and no one even stopped to ask why."

During her junior year in college, Camille met Margie. Margie reached out to her and an affectionate relationship developed. Margie didn't put demands on her—she seemed to accept her as she was. "I felt loved for the first time in my life," Camille stated. Unfortunately, the love and affection that Margie and Camille felt for each other began to be expressed in sexual ways and before long they were both struggling with the sexual confusion that resulted. Neither wanted to become a lesbian, but it was hard to turn their backs on the good feelings of love and affection. It was hard for them not to feel sexual when their needs for closeness were being met for the first time in their lives.

Leanne Payne has identified failure to receive unconditional love as one of the factors which leads to a homosexual lifestyle. She writes,

> There is never a time in a child's life when it does not need the love of a whole father and a whole mother, but apparently some stages are more critical than others for psychological health and development. . . . Much of the homosexuality we see today is the harvest sown by the breakup of the American home and the absence of whole and affirming fathers.[11]

Counselors who work with a lesbian must be ready for the possibility that their sincerity will be questioned because the counselee may not have been in a relationship in which she felt truly loved. To love your counselee means that you will keep her best interests at the forefront of counseling and that you will not do anything to hurt her. I asked one of my students if she felt her counselee would ever fall in love with her. She said, "No, she just doesn't trust me yet." In the course of counseling, however, the counselee did learn to trust her and a strong love bond was formed. From this experience of learning to give and receive love in a nonerotic way, the counselee was launched into a healing process which even resulted in a restored interest in the opposite sex.

Most lesbian counselees have difficulty differentiating between their needs for affection and their sexual needs. In fact, most seek affection—only to find that just as in their relationships with men they find sex instead. This is an important topic to discuss with your counselee. When needs for affection are only met with sex, the deep longings of the person become even more exaggerated.

Diane said, "The more I tried to find love and caring, and failed, the more needy I became. It became an obsession with me." Women need to be held just for the sake of being held, not just for sexual arousal.

Mary shared her experience. "I sat crying with my head on her shoulder and her arms tightly around me. The child in me said, *I have looked all my life for this.* After my crying subsided I began to panic. *I don't deserve this,* I said to myself. *I'm being bad.* Before long I was pulling away, afraid of being rejected and afraid that I would cause my friend to make love to me. Lucky for me she realized what was going on and began to talk to me about it. 'You are safe here,' she said. 'I won't hurt you and I won't let you hurt yourself. It is okay for you to let me hold you. I'm not going to do anything bad. Just let yourself enjoy the fact that I love you and I want to comfort you.'"

Mary was very fortunate because relationships where true comfort and affection are offered are not common. They need to be, however, because such relationships are the essence of healing for the lesbian. True affection needs to be expressed so that true healing can occur. Unfortunately, many lesbians feel they have no right to ask. They feel it is even wrong to have needs. In addition, they are afraid to share their needs with others for fear they will be seen as seductive and ultimately rejected again. Lesbians as well as other homosexuals need to learn that love and affection can be shared with limits. "I love you" does not mean that we have to become sexual lovers. Hugs do not have to lead to foreplay. When they do they lose their most valuable component, reaching out to the person. "I really care about you" heals. "I want to use you for my sexual pleasure" does not.

Within our Christian communities we need to encourage curative relationships. We need to encourage and train people not to back away from those who struggle with sexual preference. One counselee said, "As soon as the women in the Bible study learned of my problem they dropped me like a hot potato. It was like they felt I was going to pursue them and drag them into my bedroom. They stopped calling. They avoided sitting by me and if I got hugs they were certainly the abbreviated kind. All of a sudden I felt like I didn't belong. I wanted to kill myself so that I wouldn't infect anyone."

We need to teach people that they can have self-control and we need to teach them to relate to those struggling with sexual confusion just as they would relate to other people. I am not suggesting that we take huge risks when we ourselves are sexually vulnerable. I am just saying that we can choose our responses and we can teach our lesbian friends that loving, affectionate relationships do not have to be eroticized. We have been unwilling to take responsibility for our own feelings and reactions, thus thousands of people who could have been guided toward healing through our fellowship have only been pushed to further despair. This is a tragedy that needs to be reversed.

Moberly writes,

Love, both in prayer and in relationships, is the basic therapy. A defensive detachment from the same-sex love-source, and consequent unmet needs for love, constitute the homosexual condition. Love is the basic problem, the great need, and the only true solution. If we are willing to seek and to mediate the healing and redeeming love of

Christ, then healing for the homosexual will become a great and glorious reality.[12]

"I Don't Like Myself at All"

A consideration of lesbianism would not be complete without some discussion of the way in which sexual confusion and lesbian behavior affect the self-concept of the person. Lesbians are not sure of themselves. They often dislike their bodies. They live in fear of rejection. They carry deep scars of guilt which go all the way back to childhood and rejection by parents and peers. They feel different, undesirable, like Janis who said, "I don't like myself at all." All of this could be said of many people, regardless of their sexual orientation. But lesbians are aware of these feelings to a marked degree.

In discussing barriers to healing for the homosexual, Leanne Payne identifies three major ones, all of which relate to self-concept. These are, *not forgiving others, not forgiving self,* and *not receiving forgiveness from others.* Payne believes that instead of developing self-acceptance the homosexual person has turned to narcissism, or a desperate need to be the center of attention as a means of trying to realize the meeting of love needs. She uses concepts developed by Trobisch.

Self-love used in the positive sense of self-acceptance is the exact opposite of narcissism or auto-eroticism. It is actually a prerequisite for a step in the direction of selflessness. We cannot give what we do not possess. Only when we have accepted ourselves can we become truly selfless and free from ourselves. If, however, we have not found ourselves and discovered our own identity, then we must continually search for ourselves. The word *self-centered* aptly describes us when we revolve only around ourselves.[13]

"The failure to pass from the narcissistic stage on into that of self-acceptance is what we are here calling the third barrier to inner healing, the failure to accept and love oneself aright," says Payne.[14]

Lesbians and other homosexual counselees need to be taught how to love themselves. This begins with an awareness that they have value to God. He is the anchor for all proper self-esteem.

Those who are seeking to find love also need to be taught that to give is to find. Losing your life for the sake of others gives meaning to life. One of my counselees spent hours bemoaning the fact that others never seemed to want to do things for her or even to be with her. I encouraged her to move from a place of asking "why don't they love me?" to "how can I show love to them?" This is a very hard step for one who is desperate for love and acceptance, but as the step is taken, healing begins to take place. Not all people respond and reach back, but some do and relationships with these people can be the beginning of the healing process.

Another aspect of healing and self-acceptance is to teach the person to savor the positive. Most people make crumbs out of the good things they do rather than thank God for the growth and healing they are experiencing.

Pam had to learn to set goals and reach them, and then enjoy the fact that she was doing some good things for herself. I pointed out Galatians 6:4 to her.

Each one should test his own actions. Then he can take pride in himself, without comparing himself to somebody else. . . .

Pam had been so worried about being humble that she couldn't talk about anyone but herself. On the other hand, rather than enjoying the success God was empowering her to have, she ran herself down and felt worse. She couldn't accept her own accomplishments and she couldn't gain esteem from the good things others were trying to point out to her. Unfortunately, she had reduced herself to having to gain self-esteem by loving others physically. This only led to guilt which destroyed her self-esteem even more.

Try this visual aid with one of your counselees who is struggling with self-esteem. Pay her a compliment and watch for the negative response. If it comes, take a cookie (which you can place in your desk drawer before the counseling session) and give it to her. She will be confused. Without saying anything else, instruct her to crumble the cookie into a thousand pieces and then give it back to you. She will get the message. But if she doesn't, you can relate it to what she just did with your compliment. After she gets the point, give her another cookie and ask her to eat it slowly and to tell you how good it tastes. Cookie monsters are all right for "Sesame Street," but they need to be turned into savorers and compliment-appreciaters in our church fellowships.

I asked Peggy if she had to be perfect in order to accept a compliment. She struggled to answer.

"Peggy," I continued, "if I say your hair looks nice you don't have to tell me it isn't perfect. I don't care about that. I only want you to know that it looks nice to me. Please tell me thanks if you feel like it, but more important, tell yourself that it is nice to know that someone has noticed. Savor and enjoy my compliment."

Many lesbian counselees struggle with role conflicts. They find it difficult to accept themselves because they may not believe they fit what others feel the Christian woman should be. I encourage them to throw away their stereotypes and discover who they are. This includes accepting their sexual confusion and taking steps to deal with it. Self-acceptance and receiving the acceptance of others can lead to personal growth and freedom from the sexual confusion that may have resulted.

The task of helping lesbian counselees move from a place of sexual confusion and emotional disruption is a challenge for the counselor, but a challenge which should be approached with enthusiasm, not despair. As counselees' self-understanding grows they will become more willing to explore and take risks in new healing relationships. As the counselor you have the privilege of walking with your counselee along a scary path. If there are crevices along the way, at least their location can be reasonably predicted, and the landmarks are not a few. I appreciate what Barnhouse has written.

A wise teacher of mine once said, "We do not treat the patients with what we know, but with what we are." This is not to say that the years of study and experience do not provide therapists with a conceptual frame of reference which they must have in order to make sense of the confusion and irrationality which the patient presents. But no patient ever gets well because the doctor has figured out what is wrong. Patients must learn to feel differently about themselves and this can only come about through a corrective emotional experience which is based on the interpersonal transaction between the patient and the therapist. If the therapist does not really care, if the therapist is not really involved, patients continue to feel isolated and unworthy no matter how much they may have learned intellectually about the causes of such feelings.[15]

CHAPTER SIX

SPECIAL COUNSELING CONSIDERATIONS

IN MANY WAYS, COUNSELING WITH PERSONS who are struggling with homosexuality is not substantially different from other counseling interactions. In other ways, it may be vastly different. In this chapter we will look at some of the similarities and differences which you may encounter. Taking a sequential approach, we will look at special counseling considerations during each phase of the process of counseling with homosexuality.

PREPARING FOR THE INITIAL CONTACT

I often tell my counselees that the hardest part for them is getting started. In counseling with homosexuality this may be true for you as well as your counselee. If you know that the problem is homosexuality you may be fearful that you will not be able to help. Or you may be fearful of your reactions to the person. As you struggle with your agendas your counselee may be dealing with a variety of fears, questions, and general apprehension. Some counselees may never have been to a counselor. They will not know what to expect. Also, they will be fearful of not meeting your expectations. This will result in an awkward start. Some counselees have experienced so much rejection that they fear you will also reject them. You may even be able to see the apprehension written across their faces.

Bill, a counselee, said, "I had no idea what counseling would be like. For weeks before I went to see my pastor I watched him carefully and listened for any hint of what it would be like. Secretly, I hoped he would show some harshness or prejudice which would give me an excuse for not going to see him. I was comforted by his compassion for others but that didn't take away the terrible fear I harbored that he would reject me."

Little did Bill know that his pastor was going through a similar struggle. When asked about his feelings after Bill had made the appointment, the pastor replied, "I was really ambivalent. I knew Bill had been struggling for a long time and I suspected his problem was homosexuality. I wanted him to talk to me, but I felt so helpless when I tried to imagine how I might help. I wondered if my fears would show through. I asked myself if I could really offer him unconditional acceptance. I went over and over my belief about separating the sin from the sinner. At times I wanted to run. But God reminded me that he had put me in a pastoral position with Bill and I had a responsibility to give it my best. It was scary to say the least."

Preparing for a first interview with a counselee requires a combination of faith and self-control. You need faith that God will be with you regardless of the complexity of the problem. You also need confidence in yourself, your training, and your natural insights into people. It helps to remind yourself that the least you can do is extend kindness and compassion to a hurting person. Even if this is all you accomplish you will have truly given a cup of cold water to a thirsty human being (see Matthew 10:42).

Self-control comes in not allowing yourself to believe that

you have to cure the problem immediately or that you have nothing to offer. One of the people I supervised said, "What if I can't help her? What if she leaves the first session more hopeless than before?" With confidence I said, "That won't happen. You are too much of a lover of people not to make some impact. You may not 'cure' her and you may even need to make a referral at some time, but you can make an impact for good."

My supervisee looked at me skeptically and laughingly. I said, "Okay—if you can't believe or trust me, at least trust God and see what he can do."

As I prepare for an initial contact with a client which causes me uncertainty, I often rehearse some steps I want to take to insure a good start. I remind myself to be on time, to smile, and to shake hands warmly. I tell myself to listen carefully and to try to identify the personal feelings. By the time I am through with my little pep talk I usually feel confident. I realize that my checklist for counseling a homosexual is no different than the one I would need to deal with most other counseling problems. I just want to make psychological contact with people so that I can be in a position to help them share their problem and discuss their needs. Usually, as I am able to help a person tell his or her story I will be in a position to see ways in which I can be helpful.

> Openness is listening willingly to descriptions of problems that are personally threatening to us. It is easy to become anxious and defensive and try to steer the conversation to other topics. Some helpers feel nervous when talk turns to homosexuality, divorce, temptation, sexual inadequacy or even overeating. If we become anxious at the mention of a topic and prevent help seekers from discussing it, other doors of communication may close.[1]

Counselees may shock you when they relate their problem of homosexuality to you. Pray that God will give you calmness to accept whatever situations you encounter and an attitude of acceptance toward the people even if you are shocked. For example, you may be shocked when a very masculine-looking young man turns out to be a homosexual struggler. Or, you may be alarmed when a pretty mother of three announces that she is leaving her husband and children to follow her lesbian lover. In situations such as these it is always helpful to follow the rule: "If you feel like reacting, stay quiet until you get the whole story."

CONDUCTING THE INITIAL INTERVIEW

The goals of the initial interview are always the same regardless of the problem. I always strive for two things: (1) to establish a strong relationship of trust with the counselees, and (2) to reach some agreement as to the goals we will work toward in subsequent counseling sessions. Regarding the importance of the initial interview, Eisenberg and Delaney[2] write,

For the counselor, the essential process goals of the first session are to:

stimulate open, honest, and full communication about the concerns needing to be discussed and the factors and background related to those concerns

work toward progressively deeper levels of understanding, respect, and trust between self and client

provide the client with the view that something useful can be gained from the counseling sessions

identify a problem or concern for subsequent attention and work

establish the "gestalt" that counseling is a process in which both parties must work hard at exploring and understanding the client and his or her concerns

acquire information about the client that relates to his or her concerns and effective problem resolution.

I made reference earlier to my desire to help the counselee tell his or her story. I seek to do this by conveying acceptance to counselees and by showing them that I really do want to get to know and understand them. I try to ask only enough questions to help the person talk. Too many questions will turn the counseling session into an inquisition. People rarely feel comfortable when they have been grilled. The following simulated counseling interview may give you some ideas.

After receiving and glancing at an intake sheet my receptionist had given me, I found the only male in the waiting room and, approaching him with a smile and an outstretched hand, I said, "You must be Mike."

He got to his feet, shook my hand, and said, "Yes, Mike Smith."

"Come on in," I said, pointing to my office door. "You are here early so we might as well start early." Mike seemed to relax a little as he stepped toward the chair opposite my office chair.

"This is comfortable," he said as he settled in.

"Not as comfortable as mine!" I said. "But I do spend a few more hours in here than you will." He laughed and the ice seemed to be broken.

"I see you are from Portland," I said as I glanced over the intake. "Have you always lived here?"

"No," he replied, "I was born in Seattle. I came here a few years ago when I was trying to find myself."

"Tell me more about that," I said. "It sounds like you have had some big decision to make for being only twenty-two years old." (It is often helpful to forsake small talk for the sake of depth, particularly in those situations where the counselee begins to talk of struggles early in the interview. I wanted to ask what is Seattle like but that would only have taken Mike away from his concerns. In situations where the counselees seem to be avoiding issues I will stay with small talk longer and try to set them at ease with humor or discussion of things familiar to them. Sooner or later, however, I will need to lead into issues by saying something like, "It sounds like your life is pretty interesting, but it must also have some concerns. Let's talk about some of those.")

Mike continues. "Well, I have a pretty big problem. I get really confused at times." I nod and try to let Mike continue. "My parents and I had this big fight," he said. "Sometimes they just don't understand me."

I nod again and say, "That must really be difficult. Can you tell me more about it?" Mike struggles at this point and I realize he is having trouble verbalizing. "They just don't understand," he stammers, "and they yell at me like I don't even love God."

"That must really hurt," I reply. He nods and begins to cry. At this point I give him a Kleenex and wait for him to collect himself. Finally he smiles appreciatively and says, "I don't know why I do that." I reassure him by saying, "I'll make a deal with you. I won't feel strange when you cry if you won't feel strange if I cry." Once again the relationship is strengthened, but Mike still hasn't been able to verbalize the focus of his problem, his homosexual struggle. I decide it is time to press forward a little.

"Mike," I ask, "do we need to be more specific about the conflict with parents? I can work with what you have said, but it may help to get it all out on the table."

Mike nods yes but is visibly shaken when he tries to speak. Finally he says, "It's about my sexuality." I nod and wait. "I hate it," he blurts out, "but I just don't seem to help myself. I don't even know who I am." Noting that he has not yet been able to label his situation I take the risk of trying to label for him. (The reader should exercise great care not to take this step prematurely. If you guess and guess wrong the counselee may feel judged or wonder if he gave off wrong signals.)

"Mike," I said, "I sense that you are struggling with something that has affected you very deeply." He nods and I continue. "I may be wrong, but it could even be something as painful as sexual preference." He nods yes but is unable to pick up the conversation. "Perhaps you fear that you may be gay?" I query. At this point the door has been opened and he rushes through it as though it is now or never.

"I don't just fear that I am gay," he said, "I know I'm gay. I'm gay and my parents can't accept it. I know I'm breaking my mother's heart, but I don't seem to be able to help it." At this point I try to provide reassurance by telling him that I am glad he can talk to me about the struggle and that I really can see how much he is hurting.

In a typical interview the counselee would probably give a lot of general details. Sometimes all you have to say is, "Tell me as much as you want me to know about the situation." I use this kind of approach because I want to leave the responsibility and the control with the counselee. Later when I may need specific facts he will have confidence enough in me to be quite open.

I pull the initial interview to a close by clarifying expectations and by trying to reach agreement regarding future counseling activities. There are some issues that must be decided.

"Mike," I asked, "do you know why you are here? Do you seek to change or are you just wanting to understand yourself better?" Typically I get the response, "I want to change, but I don't even know if I can." I usually let counselees know that a lot of people feel that way. I empathize with Mike in his dilemma and then suggest a plan.

"That is a hard spot to be in Mike," I say. "I really appreciate your courage in hitting it head-on rather than running from it. I hope we can make some real headway."

If the response is not immediate I would continue, "I have discovered that if we can come to understand how same-sex preference has been acquired we can often determine how to help a person through it. In order to do this I will need to take a very careful history regarding your struggle. Next time, I will need to ask you a lot of details such as when you first became aware of the problem and some of your early experiences. Will you give some thought to that so you will be ready for me?" If there is no resistance I would say, "That will be a real help."

I usually conclude with two other issues: (1) a statement regarding confidentiality, and (2) a brief statement regarding my views on the causes of homosexuality and the prospects for change. Counselees must feel safe in talking to the counselor or they won't be honest. I normally say that I believe that homosexuality, like other human problems, may have many causes and we are going to search for the one that fits them best. I encourage them to remain open-minded and to assist me in the search. Only rarely are counselees uncooperative at this point.

After dealing with these issues I would close by saying something like, "Well, it sounds like we have an agreement. You will set an appointment for next week for us to continue to explore the situation. In the meantime you will think about how it all got started so it will be easier to discuss with me. It may be a lot of work, but I believe it will be well worth it for you."

——————

Embedded in this simulated initial interview are several concepts which are important to keep in mind. Use the interview as a model for structure, but do not hesitate to let the counselee talk. You will learn the most when he or she is talking.

CONDUCTING THE ASSESSMENT INTERVIEW

The topic of assessment is so important that the entire next chapter will be devoted to it. Suffice it to say at this point that your job is to observe and describe, and to elicit as much information from the counselee as possible. You will need to attend to feelings as well as facts. Don't ask why, because, most likely, your counselee will not know why.

As I talked with Mike, he volunteered this insight. "Some of the stuff I am telling you doesn't make a lot of sense to me but I am trying to describe it as best I can even if I don't understand it."

"That's all I can ask," I replied. "We'll work on what has happened for now and maybe the whys will become more apparent later."

As I go through the assessment process with the counselee I try to form tentative hypotheses regarding the relationships among various events in his or her life. *I do my best work when I don't try to push too hard to make everything fit and when I am willing to give up my first thoughts when they prove not to be helpful. Rigidity usually results in failure in both assessment and therapy.*

Another goal I have in assessment is to get the counselee involved in the process. I often ask questions such as: "Do you see any connection between this and that?" Or, "What changes did you experience after this event?" Let the counselee do the work.

Sundberg, Taplan, and Tyler have written regarding assessment:

Assessment, the information-processing part of clinical work, has three functions: decision making, image forming, and hypothesis checking. In our view clinical work always involves assessment at some point—often at several points. Even if the contact is very short, such as a ten-minute interview ending in referral elsewhere, the clinicians must gather some information that leads to a decision: they inevitably form some impression or picture of the person: and frequently they test hypotheses or guesses about the client's purposes, interests, or situation.[3]

Continuing the Change Process

Assessment and counseling are often talked about as two separate phases of the counseling process, but in reality this is not accurate. The change process may begin even before there is any counselor-counselee contact. Hans Strupp has discussed how patients may view the therapy process. He writes:

Prospective patients differ not only in the kinds of problems for which they seek help, but they show great variations in the degree of subjective distress they experience, the urgency with which they desire relief, and the eagerness with which they accept help once it is offered.

Further, they differ in their expectations of what a professional helper might do to bring about relief. Virtually everyone has retained from childhood the hope of magical solutions, a wish that becomes intensified when a person experiences anxiety and distress. In addition, there are many unrealistic expectations of what psychotherapy can do. Such expectations occur not only among uneducated or unsophisticated patients, many of whom may simply lack information; they occur, perhaps in different forms and for different reasons, among individuals who, on the basis of their education or cultural experience, have heard or read a good deal about psychotherapy. At any rate, a prospective patient's expectations may have considerable bearing on his or her approach to psychotherapy and the evolving relationship with the therapist.[4]

Persons struggling with homosexuality are in real need of hope. The phases of counseling discussed thus far should pave the way for the counselee to become more hopeful and ready to risk the discomfort of the process of counseling designed to focus on change and to work on goals. As the change process begins there is a need to continue to focus on the relationship issues cited earlier while directing the counselee toward the specific tasks which are a part of the change strategy. David Dixon refers to this stage of counseling as a task maintenance period. The counselor focuses on the task at hand while maintaining the strong relationship which is needed to facilitate the change.

Carkhuff and Berenson have called attention to the need to view the counseling process in phases.[5] The counselor seeks to move the counselee from *exploring,* through *understanding,* to *acting.*

One of the most important decisions the counselor and counselee will make is the decision regarding which goals to work on first. In working with homosexuality, I usually focus on continuing to gain understanding as a key goal. It is true that counselees want and need to change whether it is to function better or to stop engaging in self-destructive behavior, but they also need to continue to develop a bigger picture of themselves and their needs. Some counselees are quite outspoken about their change needs. Lane said,

"I've got to stop cruising. I'm killing myself. I'll go crazy if I can't stop." As I asked him about his current pattern he told me that he was spending up to eight hours per week cruising, either physically or mentally. Thus we focused upon two goals—trying to figure out in more detail how he got where he was (testing out our working hypothesis), and trying to stop his behavior.

Joanie looked at her goals differently. "I need to get my sexuality out of the center of my life," she said. "I've become so preoccupied with trying to understand myself sexually that I have stopped being a person. I don't have friends. I'm doing poorly at work and I've dropped out of church completely. I at least need to feel like I am doing something about one of these areas."

I encouraged Joanie to take on one project at a time and I helped her to identify some steps she could take. We seemed to spend time in each session checking her progress while also working on the thoughts and feelings she was having regarding her sexual struggle.

There are some specific cautions which need to be heeded in working with counseling in general, and in counseling homosexuality specifically.

1. *Goals need to be specific and tied to behavior whenever possible.* For Lane this means he kept track of the time spent cruising and considered himself successful when the total amount of time decreased. For Joanie it meant identifying specific steps in getting back with God. This was the goal she selected to start on. She began by spending time praising God for as many things as she could identify. Then later she began to have a desire to go to church.

2. *Goals need to be approached one at a time.* We all get confused when we try to do too many things at a time. I encourage my counselees to remember that the mouse ate the mountain of cheese one bite at a time.

3. *Goals should be related whenever possible so that they build on each other.* In Joanie's case her goal of getting back with God seemed to be a base for reaching another goal, that of forming new friendships.

4. *Goals need to be specified by the counselee and agreed upon by the counselor.* You can't force other people to change their values and you can't force them to accept your goals. If your counselee doesn't agree upon a goal, he or she will not follow through on the tasks you prescribe. Be very careful to see that you are headed in the same direction. Where differences are apparent don't waste time by trying to force the issue. Continue to explore and talk until you can reach agreement. Counselors often make the mistake of accepting tentative words of agreement, such as "I guess so" or a hesitant Okay as a commitment. When you sense hesitation do not proceed until you are sure that you and your counselee are committed to the same action.

5. Lastly, *goals need to be significant to counselees but not so extensive that they are unreachable.* Part of the genius of

103

counseling is to help counselees target goals that are large enough for them to feel they are going somewhere, but small enough for them to feel confident that they can be reached.

Sally was the kind of person who felt she had to climb Mt. Everest in one day. When we started to talk about goals she began to panic because she felt like she had to do everything at once. She wanted to break off her relationship with her lover, establish new friendships, and work on healing with her parents all at once.

Realizing what she was about to do to herself, I said, "Oh Sally, you forgot something. I want you to establish relationships with at least two men this week also."

She gave me a look of helplessness for just a minute and then she caught my grin. As she relaxed I started to laugh.

"Sally," I said, "how about letting up on yourself and finding some success rather than pressuring yourself and not being able to reach any of your goals?" We talked some more and she decided she would start by writing a letter to her lover in which she would tell her she was *choosing* to break off the relationship. I stressed the need to say good-bye in a way she could stick to. She asked if I would read it before she sent it and I said we could do that first thing next session. We now had a workable beginning and Sally felt confident even though she was afraid. Those who set goals carefully, thoughtfully, and realistically usually experience the joy of reaching them.

Dealing with the Ups and Downs of Progress

Progress in counseling, especially with a problem as complex as homosexuality, is never a straight line between two points. It is usually a curved line, sometimes one that resembles the waves on the ocean or the trajectory of a roller coaster. If you do not help your counselees to anticipate these ups and downs they may become discouraged and lose hope.

Darren said, "Just when I thought I was getting somewhere I fell flat on my nose. If you hadn't prepared me for that I know I would have run."

There are some common pitfalls which you can help your

counselee anticipate. The following list, although not complete, will help you to get started.

1. *Fear of failure.* Don was very enthusiastic when he first started counseling. He had wanted to change his life for a long time. His initial contacts with his counselor were positive and he was actually excited about his appointment each week. The counselor could hardly believe it when he did not show up for the fourth appointment. It was even more surprising that he didn't call. Finally, the counselor called him and asked him to return, at least to explain what was going on. Don's answer was short and simple.

"I froze!" he said. "I wanted so much to succeed for you and for me and I just became terrified that I would only fail." The counselor's response was right on target.

"Don," he said, "you will probably have more moments of failure. Those rough times are pretty predictable. My job is to help you keep your eyes off the failures and on the successes. How about starting over? You won't win every battle, but you will move forward." Don's response was one of great relief. He hadn't wanted to quit in the first place but fear can do some strange things to us all.

2. *Fear of success.* Barbara started very slowly in counseling. She was depressed and confused. After a time things began to click for her and she began to have a sense of hope. Her mind was active and her enthusiasm began to grow. One day, however, she seemed depressed again. The old Barbara had returned. As we talked she said, "I don't think I can do it. I just don't think I have what it takes."

At first I thought she was afraid to fail, but as we talked I realized that was not it. She was actually afraid of success. She was finally able to say, "I know how to hurt myself and I know how to be sad but I don't know how to be happy. If I let myself open up to people and to new relationships I don't know what it will be like."

I assured her that it was okay to feel fearful. I also assured her that she could learn how to experience the joys of normal life. I offered her the support she needed.

"Barbara," I said, "I'm going to help you to learn that you

don't have to fail in order to be happy. We often get comfortable with our pain and it feels less scary than the new ways we are learning. In the long run, however, you will feel the best as you progress."

As a counselor, don't be afraid to challenge your counselees to be all they can be even though they may panic at times over their success.

3. *Wanting to return to the familiar.* During a lull in one of our sessions I said, "Darrell, you are kind of distant today. Do you have any idea what is going on?"

He thought for a while but couldn't come up with anything. "I'm just restless," he said. "I don't know what is going on."

"Let me tell you what happens to some people," I said. "If it fits, fine; but if it doesn't fit just say so." He nodded and I continued. "Your life may feel like it doesn't really fit right now. It is all strange and new. Your discomfort may be related to feelings of loss of the familiar. Even though you don't want your old lifestyle back, there may still be a pull in that direction. You may have a real pull to go back to the life you knew for so long. What do you think?" I was close to what Darrell was feeling and this opened up a whole new area of exploration. I was able to help him get free from his guilt over being pulled by the past and to move forward in commitment to his new lifestyle. Later, he told me that it was helpful to know that he was not evil or abnormal to want to go back, especially in view of his *real desire* to keep going forward. Ambivalence is a very common feeling during counseling. You will do well to help your counselees recognize that being drawn to the familiar doesn't mean they can't keep going forward.

4. *Return of old temptations.* The tug of the past may not always be harmless. Sometimes your counselees will become almost obsessed with the need to return to their old life. One counselee told me that for two days she had struggled with the desire to call an old lover. She would pick up the telephone and then put it down again. Within a few minutes the struggle would begin again. The battle was beyond anything she had ever imagined.

When old temptations return, your counselees need your strong support. Let them know that you are there for them because you want them to win. The longer they can avoid temptation the weaker it will become. This does not mean, however, that it will not be overwhelming at times. Use the onslaught of old temptations as an occasion to explore new feelings and to learn of old connections which may need to be broken.

Dan said, "I just don't understand it. For the last week I have been overwhelmed with the desire to be with a man." He couldn't think of anything that could have caused it. He even wondered about demon possession. I do not deny that demons have an interest in counselees' failures, but in Dan's case we traced the problem to a telephone call from his father. Dan had thought the conversation had gone okay but as we analyzed it his dad had dropped several bombshells which had hit the target without Dan knowing it. Once more, Dad had succeeded in getting the message across: "Dan, you will never please me. You will never be a man."

Dan's subconscious response was a return of the longing for male approval. His overt response was to want sexual contact with a male. As this became clear to him he became angry with his dad as well as angry with himself. We worked through the anger and Dan finally resolved not to let Dad's destructive messages defeat him. As he did this the intensity of the old temptations began to decrease and Dan felt back in control again.

Counselors need to exercise care not to panic when their counselees are tempted; rather, you must work carefully with them to avoid the temptation when possible. If your counselees fall back into old sinful patterns, encourage them to start over. You may have to help them to remember again the truth of 1 John 1:9 and to realize that they are as free from the guilt of the newest sin as they are from the sins they committed prior to counseling. They may need to know that you have forgiven them as well as God. Your approval or disapproval, your forgiveness or lack of forgiveness may be interpreted as the attitude of God. It is an awesome responsibility; so ask God for the ability to encourage your counselee away from sin without withdrawing your love when he or she falls. Worthington writes:

One of the most difficult attitudes for many Christians to maintain is acceptance. Because God told people things in the Scriptures that are true, Christians often treat as worthless a person who does not agree with that truth. We know that Jesus told us to love even our enemies (Lk 6:27). We know that he exhorted us not to condemn a person regardless of his or her sins (Jn 8:2–11). Yet we have a hard time practicing our beliefs. Perhaps that is why we are commanded often throughout Scripture to refrain from judging. When we accept a person we might disagree entirely with his or her beliefs. We might even believe that the person's actions are self-destructive. But we continue to value our friend and his or her right to consider the behavior to be reasonable, even when we disapprove.[6]

5. *What about new sin?* Counselees often have a belief that if they get one area under control they will fall into a new pattern of sin. This may become a self-fulfilling prophecy for some of your counselees. If they think they will fail, they usually will. As a counselor you will need to help your counselees receive forgiveness for new sin as well as old and to move forward in expectation of God's forgiveness and deliverance.

Shortly after Sally terminated a lesbian relationship she got involved with a man who used her sexually. She felt terribly guilty about this and was also hurt by the negative experience.

"How could I have been so stupid," she cried. "I don't think God will ever forgive me."

We talked a long time about God's mercy and his willingness to forgive. Sally finally came to realize that the hardest part of the forgiveness might be her coming to a place where she could forgive herself.

"I think I was trying to prove a point," she said, "but I really didn't prove anything but how rotten men are and how sinful I am." It took quite a while to work through all the problems created by the new sin but Sally eventually experienced forgiveness and healing that she initially thought was impossible.

6. *Perfectionism.* Many counselees ask, "What can I expect of counseling? Will I be totally healed?" My initial response is

usually the same. "I don't know. Right now let's just take things as far as we can and try not to limit God."

As counseling goes along, however, many counselees get discouraged with themselves and with the process. Those who are the most perfectionistic seem to have the most trouble accepting the small steps of progress which may be evident. If you as the counselor do not deal with this issue your counselee may experience a painful down spell. Your job is to stick with your clients through the periods of discouragement caused by their perfectionism and to keep them focused upon their goals and the progress they have made toward those goals.

Over and over again I found myself saying, "Sure, Stuart, you'd like to be perfect but you aren't going to be. I'm sorry, but you are a child of the King, not the King himself. We can praise God for progress—we don't have to wait for perfection."

I usually tell counselees that they may never be completely free from their homosexual struggles. In fact, I encourage them to set a goal of being able to live a normal, self-controlled life which is not to be confused with a life without sexual temptation. Stuart found it helpful to realize that heterosexual men also struggle with sexual temptation. We are all called to obedience.

7. *Plateaus.* It is great to climb a mountain and feel the fresh breeze as you rest on top. It is more difficult, however, when you have reached a level on the mountain and can't seem to get to the next level. Sometimes counselees stay at the same level for months. They hit plateaus that seem to go on forever. For some this is a dangerous period because they feel discouraged and aren't sure they will ever make progress again. When counselees are "plateaued" I usually help them find some new ways of looking at what is happening in their lives. Sometimes they are actually being strengthened as time goes by. Other times they are learning how to handle old situations in new ways. They may also be expecting spectacular changes when such changes are not in the offing. You will be the most helpful when you keep the attention on what has been and is going on, rather than allow the counselee to see the plateau as a catastrophe.

I often follow the mountain-climbing analogy and remind

the counselees that when they climb they need the flat spots in order to rest and set their strategy for the next climb. This sometimes helps counselees to feel okay with where they are so that they don't sabotage their situation by running or trying to run before they can walk.

8. *Return of previously "resolved" issues.* Stuart, the perfectionist mentioned above, came to a session totally devastated because some issues he thought he had resolved had suddenly reappeared.

"I can't go on!" he said. "I just can't do it. You worked for three months to get me over my anger toward my dad and now it is back again."

"Wait! Wait! Wait!" I said. "Who got you over that anger? If I did it no wonder it didn't last. You did it and you can do it again." I reminded Stuart that relearning is always faster than the original process and that this new development was an opportunity for relearning. He wasn't impressed at first, but slowly he saw that what I had said is true. The key thing was keeping him from going into a period of regression which would undo most of the progress we had made.

Issues may come up several times during the course of counseling. This does not mean that they have not been dealt with. It only means that they are difficult and resistant to change. Use the reappearance of the old issues as an occasion to rehearse the success of the past—the plans and the new perceptions which had brought relief in the first place. In some cases the return of old issues may be helpful because that will set the occasion for dealing with the old problem at a newer level. I use the analogy of peeling an onion, layer by layer. This has been an encouragement to counselees, especially as they are led to new progress. Try to help your counselees see each step in counseling, even the recurrence of old issues as opportunities for greater healing rather than evidence of past failures.

9. *Emergence of unexpected emotion.* Most people are afraid of their emotions, especially when they don't understand them. Unexpected emotions may be negative or positive—fear, anger, hatred, or hurt are common, as are feelings of love, affection, or joy, when depression begins to lift. Whatever the

feelings, they may send the counselee into a panic if he or she is not used to that feeling.

Recently, I interviewed a person who could not identify many feelings. Although my questions were not particularly probing they did serve to open the doors to all kinds of feelings of which the counselee had not previously been aware. For this counselee, the experience was very positive and much growth resulted. For others, the experience has been the opposite. Regardless of the emotions which emerge, the counselor must be ready to help the counselee walk through them.

I follow a three-step process: awareness, evaluation, and disposition. I believe emotions are like vital signs. They tell us when something is wrong or when changes are taking place. I encourage counselees to spend some time just observing and feeling. After the counselee is aware of what emotions are there, he or she can focus on understanding the reason for the emotion and the effect it is having on the person. When the evaluation is complete the counselee needs to decide what to do with the emotions. I call this disposition. We cannot choose what we feel, but we can choose what to do with the feelings we have. We can choose which emotions to savor and which to set aside. As counselees learn that they have choices regarding emotions they are helped to avoid the down periods which may accompany new feelings. Emotions must be dealt with as they arise. Even though it may seem comfortable to set them aside, this avoidance tactic does not work.

10. *Surfacing of repressed material.* Just as emotions may appear unexpectedly, so may a new awareness of events of the past. Your counselees may remember facts or details from the past which are quite upsetting.

Lane became very upset when he became aware that he had had homosexual contact while in grade school. He had told me before that there had been no such contact. His initial response to the new information was fear and panic, as he couldn't understand what it all meant. His greatest need was to talk about the new information until he could integrate it into his previous understanding of himself. Many questions arose, but eventually Lane arrived at a more accurate picture of himself and his problem.

111

———————————

Sometimes the material which surfaces may be very confusing for the counselee. Dan believed that he had never been aroused by women. This was the foundation for his belief that he was "born a homosexual." When he remembered being aroused by girls in junior high school he became very upset, and after talking it over and clarifying the memories he began to challenge his assumption that *he could not change*. This new awareness led him to hope for a future which he had previously not thought possible.

After the initial assessment with counselees and after some time in counseling I often ask counselees to review their recollections to see if there is anything new. Problems as complex as homosexuality often result in repression or confusion of memories. The counselor's job is to help the counselee get a picture of the past which is as clear as possible.

Working with persons with problems of same-sex preference is always a challenge, but attention to the issues discussed above will enable the counselor to interact with the counselee in more effective and efficient ways. The process of counseling with homosexuality will be served best by a thorough but patient approach by which the counselor deals with each issue from the perspective of a solid relationship with the counselee.

CHAPTER SEVEN

ASSESSING COUNSELEE NEEDS

WHEN A PERSON WALKS INTO YOUR OFFICE and says, "I want your help," it can mean anything. The person may be upset and not know why. He or she may be in the midst of a moral crisis. There may be a struggle over identity. Decisions may need to be made. You may discover that what the person says is the problem may not turn out to be the problem at all.

When I ask a counselee why he or she has come to see me and the answer is, "Because I'm a homosexual" or, "Because I'm having some sexual problems," I am careful not to jump to conclusions. The next question I ask is usually, "Can you help me to understand your struggle a little better?" This is the beginning of the assessment process.

Jill said, "I'm just attracted to women. That's all. I think there must be something wrong with me. I want to be held all the time." At that point, neither Jill nor I was able to say what the real problem was. She burst into tears as she said, "I'm afraid I'm a homosexual! Am I?"

"I don't know," I said as compassionately as possible. "I guess you are here so I can help you to answer that haunting question."

At this point Jill was ready to approach the hard work of understanding herself, her behavior, her choices, her thoughts, and her feelings.

Bob's situation was different. He had not been in my office five minutes before he said, "I have got to stop living like this—I'm destroying everything that I value—my wife, my children, my Christian testimony—even my job." Bob was practicing homosexuality. He was lunging frantically down a path of self-destruction. In his case, the purpose of the assessment is to understand *why* in order to direct him toward some alternative patterns.

I believe if we as counselors can help clients who are struggling with issues related to homosexuality realize what they are doing and how they have come to the place of doing it, then we can help them change directions. If we know how behavior was learned, it is easier to help the person unlearn it. That process of helping people to change will be discussed in later chapters. At this point we will focus upon understanding the person and his or her problem, and then on turning those understandings into a plan for helping the person.

CATEGORIES OF PROBLEMS

I have found it helpful to realize that most of the counselees who come to me with questions related to homosexuality usually fall into one of five categories. We will consider the categories in the order of increasing sexual involvement, from undefined sexuality to bisexual pleasure-seeking.

Undefined sexuality is a term I use to denote those persons who do not seem to be interested in sex in what they consider a normal way and therefore feel that there must be something wrong with them. If they have done much reading they may wonder if they are latent homosexuals. Jim said, "Girls just don't interest me. I don't know what's wrong. All the other guys are going out and having a good time, but I just don't seem to be able to get into it." When I asked Jim about his experiences with men he said, "I like them, but I don't have any close friends. I think I'm afraid they will think I'm weird. I don't have any sexual stories to tell like they do."

I responded, "You mean you can't brag in the locker room about all your sexual exploits?"

"That's right," he said. "The most exciting thing I ever did was hold a girl's hand at a movie."

I asked Jim about his attraction to men. "I admire them," he said. "I sometimes wish I was like them. I like to be around them, but I don't know whether it is sexual." Jim's only sexual experience had been a time of mutual masturbation in which he and his friend Bill had engaged at about age thirteen. "That has bothered me a lot," he said. "We almost got caught and I really was afraid. I don't know whether we were being homosexual or not. We didn't touch each other. I felt so guilty I haven't done it since."

Jim's fear of being considered abnormal and his fear of getting caught had resulted in his repressing his normal sexual desires and trying to remain sexless. He had come to me because he was beginning to lose the battle and could no longer keep his feelings down. He had to know what was wrong.

Phillip Swihart has discussed the problem of repression:

Repression comes at great cost for it saps our energies like a hidden short in an electrical system. It takes effort to keep these feelings hidden in the recesses of our unconscious. As a child, did you ever play with a bit of wood or a balloon, trying to push it under the surface of a tank of water? It was fun and fascinating because it was so difficult to keep it from floating to the surface. Keeping down feelings that we fear will blow up in our face or reveal us as some kind of monster is an energy drain that leaves us less able to help others and to be about the King's business in general.

The dishonesty of repression not only robs us of

emotional, physical and spiritual energy, of a full life, but it also hinders the healing of emotional wounds.[1]

Jim's energies had been sapped and he could no longer put forth the effort to deny his sexuality. It had to be defined and it had to be defined now. He was fearful of losing his mind. I felt it was important to ease Jim's tension even before I took him through the assessment interview which will be presented below.

I said, "Jim, are you a latent homosexual?" He squirmed uneasily as I used the words. "I don't know," he said, "but I am really afraid."

"I don't believe in such a thing," I said with a smile. "I judge homosexuality by behaviors and you haven't acted that way. I think the choice is still yours. Shall we find out?" He nodded with some enthusiasm and we made plans to continue the process of defining himself sexually.

Margaret's story illustrates the second category—*sexual confusion*. She seemed to be getting conflicting messages from her brain. Her emotions were like an electrical system with a short. One moment they were on, the next minute they were off. "I don't know what I want," she said. "When I'm with some of my close girlfriends I want to be close to them and I do seem to respond sexually. On the other hand I have been attracted to guys. I'm just a mess. I can't form close relationships with either because I'm afraid I'll end up being the other way."

I queried, "Do you mean if you relate sexually to women you're afraid that might be a mistake because you might not be a homosexual, and if you relate sexually to men, you are afraid that might be a mistake because down deep you might be gay?" She shook her head yes and the tears began to flow. It was clear that she felt that whatever she did would turn out wrong.

I proceeded by saying, "Let's pretend for a while that neither label is correct. In fact, let's put the labels aside and just explore what you think and feel when you're with men and what you experience with women. We can't label when we can't even describe."

This process freed Margaret to sort through her confusion and begin to understand the various pressures she was feeling. "Maybe," I said hopefully, "you will find that you have more control over this situation than you realize." "I certainly hope so," she replied. "I can't stand this roller coaster."

In assessing counselees with sexual confusion I have found several problem areas. First, they are not usually able to distinguish between normal needs for affection and sexual desire. During the assessment interview I asked Margaret, "What do you think you want most from Diane?" After some thought she said, "I don't really like the thought of her making love to me, but I really like to be hugged and held by her. Sometimes I don't want her to let me go." This difference was crucial in clarifying the sexual-preference issue for Margaret.

People who suffer from sexual confusion also have difficulty distinguishing between sexual thoughts and sexual behavior. Mark asked, "Am I a homosexual? The other night I woke up dreaming that Dan was touching my penis." I avoided a premature conclusion.

"I don't know, Mark," I said. "Does a dream make a person anything?"

Curiosity also creates sexual confusion. Julie said, "She started to touch my breasts and I didn't stop her. I guess I just wanted to know what it would feel like. When I liked it then I really got upset. I didn't know what to think, but I knew I better try to figure it out."

In order to try to decrease the panic, I often help the person to see the normal aspects of the situation. "Julie," I asked, "did God make women's breasts sensitive to touch or not?"

"I guess so," she responded. "He certainly did mine."

"If your breasts are pleasure-sensitive," I continued, "then why would you expect it to be different if they were being touched by a woman?"

"I don't know," she said. "I just know it was weird and I didn't like the way I felt afterward." I assured Julie that it was okay to be confused and that we would explore the matter until she felt more in control once again. Curiosity often contributes to sexual confusion but it need not lead to changes in sexual preference.

Walt came to me for counseling, realizing that he had a definite *sexual preference.* "As much as I hate to admit it," he said, "the truth is I am turned on by men and not by women. I just can't understand it—no one else in my family is this way." When questioned, Walt revealed that his sexual preference for men went back to puberty. He stated that he could not remember ever being sexually aroused by a woman. Others like Walt have a preference for men but report that they have been aroused by women and may even have had some sexual encounters with the opposite sex.

It is important to have counselees remember as much detail as possible about their experiences in order to assess whether or not the tendencies may be reversible. In my experience, counselees have told me of remembering interactions with the opposite sex which they had put out of their minds. Darrel thought he had never been aroused by a woman, but discovered that he had gotten aroused and tried to make love to a girl when he was a high-school sophomore. She had rejected him and told him that he would never be a man. This experience turned out to be pivotal in his beliefs about his sexuality. Shortly after this event he began to interpret all of his experience as though he were a homosexual. To use my terminology, *the filter,* "I am a homosexual" was firmly in place. (See chapter 4.)

Filters not only affect the counselees' interpretation of current interaction; they can also affect the way a person interprets past experience. In Darrel's case he didn't interpret his past heterosexual involvement at all. He just filtered it out. He was extremely surprised when this was pointed out to him.

When a definite sexual preference is reported, the function of the assessment process is to help both counselor and counselee to understand factors which may have contributed to the preference so that decisions about behavior can be made. In some cases, as was stated in chapter 4, the preference may suggest some biochemical involvement, while in other cases the pattern of learned preference can be clearly traced. This information is of utmost importance to the counselees who are trying to decide upon a lifestyle and are trying to relate their choice of lifestyle to other aspects of their lives, such as their belief system. I always believe counselees when they say they have a definite sexual preference, but I never assume that that preference is as unchangeable as the counselees believe it to be.

Homosexual pleasure seeker is another category I often use to describe counselee behavior. Don, a prominent businessman in the Midwest, asked to see me when I visited his state. He had been caught in the act of fellatio* with a man in a public restroom. The legal aspects of the case had been dealt with but Don's problem was his fiancée. She had been shocked at the news and their relationship was in serious jeopardy. They were both confused and in need of some answers.

Don's claim that he was not a homosexual was met by more skepticism from me than from his fiancée. She told me, "I don't know what to think. I do know that he gets sexually excited by me. We haven't had sex because of our beliefs, but I think we could. I really love him and I don't want to walk away if there is any hope of a normal marriage."

As I assessed the situation with Don I discovered that he had grown up with strong taboos about premarital sex. He had not only memorized 1 Corinthians 7:1b (KJV), "It is good for a man not to touch a woman"; that truth had been indelibly imprinted across his thoughts and behavior. As Don's sexual desires began to arise they had no outlet because he could not allow himself to think of the normal outlet—sex with a woman. He started involving himself with sexual pleasure through masturbation. Interestingly, he did so without thinking of either men or women; he just mechanically played with himself until he experienced pleasure. His first homosexual encounter happened by accident—someone asked to touch him and make him feel good, and he let them. This later expanded to other forms of pleasure between Don and other men, and he was hooked. He became an addict to sexual pleasure, and was highly active until he got caught. He never really considered his activity sexual—to him it was simply pleasure. "Until I wound up in jail," he said, "I never let myself think of what I was doing as sex. Sex was something I didn't let myself think of because I wasn't married."

After a thorough assessment I concluded that Don was not a

---

* Fellatio: providing oral sex for a man.

119

homosexual and that he could probably function as a marriage partner. I warned both him and his fiancée that he might continue to struggle with homosexual lust after marriage. Sexual obsessions are not easily broken. They did marry and with the aid of counseling and the grace and mercy of our God they have had a happy, normal life together.

Pleasure seekers represent a large percentage of the homosexual population. Although fear of AIDS has begun to decrease their numbers, obsession with anonymous sex has gripped literally thousands of males. Pleasure without commitment has been a driving force for many. Persons who fall into this category need help in breaking the mental bondage under which they have fallen. Addiction to sexual pleasure is just as real as addiction to marijuana or cocaine.

I use the term *bisexual pleasure seekers* to refer to individuals who, like the homosexual pleasure seekers, are addicted to sexual pleasure. There is a difference however; the bisexual will give and receive pleasure from either sex. I sometimes encounter Christians who are married and have children and are still having sexual encounters with people besides their spouses.

"I guess it is adultery," one man said, "but I never think of it in that way. I love my wife very much, but I just have a high sex drive. Those other people don't mean anything to me."

Two factors seem to be prominent: obsession with pleasure and the excitement associated with the hunt. Joe said, "I think fear keeps me going as much as anything. I'm pumped up emotionally. I'm excited about who I will find and I even think there is some excitement over the possibility of getting caught. Sometimes sex at home is too safe to be fun."

I believe Joe not only suffers from sexual obsession but is also a drug addict. His drug is hormones. The fear of getting caught turns him on and he repeats the pattern day after day. If he is going to survive he needs careful counseling and supervision to break the addiction and learn a whole new pattern of life.

Other bisexuals are not as trapped. Their addiction may just be approval, or they may never have learned self-control. In either case they will not be cured by injunction. Telling them to stop will not change their behavior. They need to be led through a process of retraining.

These five categories are not intended to be all-inclusive. They are merely suggestions which may help you to better understand what is going on with those whom you counsel. The categories are not as important as the description of the actual thoughts and behaviors which the counselee is experiencing. Understanding what the person is experiencing is more important than labeling him or her. Once you can clearly understand *what,* you are in a position to search for *why,* and the possibilities for change. The assessment interview guideline which follows can help you as a counselor to explore the client's experience in depth. The interview is based upon the assumption that sexual behavior and sexual preference are affected by several factors: parent-child relationships, observations of parents' sexual behavior, early sexual experiences, and biochemical factors which can only be inferred.

BASIC ASSESSMENT INTERVIEW

Each of the following items needs to be covered, although the order may not be important. If I deal with a talkative counselee, I may let him or her set the pace and volunteer information. Care must be taken, however, to be thorough and not to let counselees skip over important information.

1. *Explore clients' relationship with parents.*

Ask specific questions about how they related to both mother and father and stepparents, if there were any. I ask questions such as, How did your mother or father show you they loved you? I also question them about either verbal or sexual abuse. Other productive questions might be, What is your fondest memory of your mother (or father)? What is the most disappointing thing you remember? I ask how each parent disciplined and how each parent made them feel either good or bad. I also ask how they feel their parents treated them in comparison to their siblings (if applicable).

Two questions are of particular importance and should never be left out: To men, I say, How did your father make you feel like a man? And, How did your mother make you feel like a man? The same questions should be asked of a female counselee with the emphasis upon how each parent made her feel feminine. These questions will often be answered, "They didn't." When I get this answer I ask, "How did they make you feel then?"

As I listen to the counselees' responses I begin to formulate notions about how the parent-child interaction may have affected the person. Answers such as "my dad always implied that I would never be a man," may reveal where the learning of homosexual tendencies began.

2. *Ask about the counselees' observations of their parents' relationship with each other*, including their sexual relationship. Answers such as "my parents were never close" or, "they always fought a lot about sex" may suggest reasons for the counselee becoming fearful of normal sexual contact. One counselee's only memory was of his mother pushing his father away. From that he learned to question whether or not a man's sexual needs could ever be met by a woman. Later, as a teenager, when he was pushed away by a girl, he stopped thinking of women as sexually desirable. If I ask counselees about their memories of parents during the initial or second interview, I always ask them to keep thinking about it until the next week so that they can add more recollections. Some of the most important things may be what they remember later.

3. *Ask counselees to give a detailed account of their sexual history with the same sex and with the opposite sex.* I usually ask my counselees to try to do this in chronological order and I write it down in detail. If they say, for example, that they were never attracted to the opposite sex, I push for more detail. "When was the first time you realized little girls and little boys were different? Who was your first girlfriend? Did you ever wish you knew how to make love to a woman?"

Counselees will often overlook details and, sometimes, entire incidents. I press them to stretch their memories. They often recall key events between counseling sessions.

As I go through the histories with them I try to look for key factors that may have led to the development of a filter that said, "I am a homosexual" or, "I am not attracted to the opposite sex." Somewhere in this assessment I explain the filtering process and ask them to try to look for ways they may have filtered certain material. At that point I usually try to pull together ideas from each of the three main areas: parent-child relationship, early observations of parents, and their own sexual experience.

Here is an example from an assessment interview.

"Jack," I said, "during the last three meetings we have talked about a lot of things that may have affected how you feel sexually. I want to summarize the key points to see if you can see how they may have affected you.

"First, your dad gave the message that you weren't a man. This was coupled with your mom's lack of affection which caused you not to be drawn to women. You wanted love from Dad more than love from Mom." He agreed and I continued.

"Somewhere during this process you began to be attracted to other boys and you experienced sexual excitement for the first time when you saw another boy in the shower and his penis was erect. You even said you wished you could be like him. In the meantime you were afraid of girls and didn't go out for fear they would make fun of you. Your father made it worse when he said, 'You don't date, so maybe you aren't a man. I sure hope you aren't a queer or something.'

"Wasn't it shortly after that that you began to see yourself as strange and became more and more interested in males? You also said a forward girl had approached you, but you denied your excitement by telling yourself that you could never please her anyway. This filter led you to your first sexual encounter with a male, and although it made you physically ill you repeated it because you had been excited and you had a feeling that for the first time in your life you had pleased a man."

It took Jack a long time to process all that I had said, but as he did so it made sense to him. It seemed like a plausible explanation of his same-sex preference. I wrote down the main points and asked him to think about them and evaluate them for a while. In the next session we clarified a few points and added new information. When he was satisfied and I was satisfied that we knew how his same-sex preference had been learned we were ready to tackle the next step—unlearning.

Assessment is an ongoing process which continues right on

through counseling. Each insight gained adds to one's understanding of the past, present, and future. I do not always provide the interpretation of the data for the counselee. Sometimes I will ask, "Do you see any possible relationship between your need for affection and your attraction to people of the same sex?" When counselees perceive things for themselves they often grow the most rapidly in their understanding.

There are many other questions that could be asked. You will need to follow the leads which the counselees give to you. If female counselees talk about an interest in trucks, or male clients talk about an interest in dolls, I listen. There may be valuable information there. I write down all the information I get, for I may hold the key to understanding a person and eventually setting him or her free.

OTHER ASSESSMENT TOOLS

Although I rely heavily upon the information gained from the type of interview described above, I don't hesitate to use psychological tests or sexual inventories to provide additional information. If you are trained to use such instruments, do so. They may provide insight. If you have counselees you can't understand you may want them to have psychological evaluations. The results of the evaluations can help you as you counsel with them. Working closely with other counselors may be helpful.

Insights from peers and parents may also add to your understanding of counselees. When information is volunteered, use it. When it is not volunteered, respect the wishes of the counselees and get their permission before talking to others.

Finally, have your counselee keep a journal and bring it in to you each week. I ask counselees to record childhood memories, dreams, and current feelings and experiences. These journals not only serve a valuable assessment function, but also help counselees see changes that are taking place in them. This often serves as an aid in the fight against depression, for it helps them see progress.

Assessment Includes a Plan

As you learn about the counselee you will need to work with him or her to set goals and to work toward these goals. Success or failure with a specific goal is also useful assessment. When the person fails you, try to figure out why. When the person succeeds you evaluate the meaning which that success has upon future learning. Assessment is not historical and stagnant. It is ongoing and dynamic. The more skilled you become at assessment the better plans you and the counselee will be able to develop. Work at developing the skills mentioned above. It is a challenging and fascinating process.

CHAPTER EIGHT

CONDUCTING THE ASSESSMENT INTERVIEW

IN THE PREVIOUS CHAPTER I discussed the assessment process and the reader was advised of problems which may be encountered and objectives to pursue. In this chapter, assessment will be discussed practically, not theoretically. How do you get the information you need in order to understand your counselees and develop intervention strategies which are appropriate for them? Guessing is not good enough. Wherever possible we need to *know*.

Assessment is a process which is not as simple as drawing blood or taking a temperature. In most cases we are dealing with the memory of past feelings and events which may not be very reliable. I have discovered that many of my counselees do

126

not remember some very significant events until several sessions into the counseling process.

I had counseled with Aaron every other week for six months. During the more formal assessment interviews he had indicated that when he had dated he had never been sexually aroused by his female dates. One day he spontaneously said, "Do you remember when we talked about me dating Susan?" I nodded yes. "I just remembered something," he continued. "I remembered a conversation I had with her about going too far. The more I thought about that the more I realized that I had really been turned on. I guess I had forgotten it because of the other experiences when I hadn't been turned on."

This new data allowed Aaron and me to look at some possibilities for his interaction with females which had not previously been available. It might not have come up, however, had the assessment interviews not been thorough enough to cover his dating behavior and stir up new thoughts about the past. Counselees may be so wrapped up in their current feelings that they wall off memories of the past. This is particularly true if they have developed filters which tend to interpret all data from the perspective: "I am a homosexual so those things couldn't have happened to me."

Assessment with the homosexual counselee must always be kept dynamic. In one sense the counselor can never be satisfied with the answers acquired. I find myself constantly saying "tell me more." "What were some of the other feelings you had at that time? Are there any events you have forgotten?" Questions of this type tend to stir the counselees to think while they are not in your presence, just as they have to think when you are interviewing them.

PREPARING THE COUNSELEE FOR ASSESSMENT

Just as doctors and nurses prep their patients for surgery we have to prepare our counselees for assessment. At the end of the initial interview I usually say, "During the next couple sessions I am going to need to get to know as much about you as I possibly can. The better I understand you and the more I know of your history, the more precise I can be in helping you deal with your life. Can you stand nosey people? . . . I'll try not to be obnoxious, but I will want details. You probably won't know the answers to everything I ask but that is okay. When you remember things or do come up with answers, write them down and give them to me later." Counselees do best when you take the pressure off them to have to remember perfectly. You will also have to give them permission to correct previous answers as they think through the various topics addressed.

When Jacque came to the second assessment interview, she said, "I don't think I had everything straight last time. I told you I had not had any contact with females prior to high school. As I thought about it I remember that my Aunt Mildred— Dad's sister—used to sleep with me when she would visit. She always slept nude and she would ask me to take off my pajamas. I didn't think anything of it but I remember that she did touch me and kiss me sometimes and she used to call me her cuddly little teddy bear."

This new information proved to be very vital as it helped Jacque to see how she had first realized that she could make women happy. This, coupled with the fact that she had been forced and hurt sexually by her first boyfriend, helped her to realize where the lesbian leaning may have begun. Keep your counselees' memories alive and be sure to give them time to share new insights with you. Do not rush through the assessment stage.

Another part of preparing your counselees for assessment is to let them know how you use the information. You don't want them sitting there wondering, "if I tell him this what will he think?" or "what will she do with all this?"

After an assessment interview in which my counselee had said to herself, *Okay, let's get honest here,* she asked me, "What did you think of me last time? Did I ruin our relationship?" We had covered the topic before but she needed reassurance. I tried humor.

"Well," I replied, "I did just what I told you I would do. I bought space in the newspaper and I'm telling the whole world everything that has happened to you!" She relaxed a little and then said, "Seriously now, what did you do with all that? Do you think I am a terrible person?"

At this point I needed to make an honest disclosure of myself if the assessment process was to continue. I decided to cover three areas—the abuse against her, her sin, and how I choose to view people.

"Let's start with the things that have been done to you," I said. "It hurt me to know that you have had to go through all that pain. I realized it is not surprising that you are sexually confused." We talked about this area for a while.

"Now," I said, "let me give you my view on the wrong things that you have done." Tension really returned at this point. "I believe that we all have to be responsible for our sins, but that God wants us to be forgiven sinners, free from the past. I'll make a deal with you—I won't hold those past sins against you if you won't hold my past against me." She nodded okay and I said, "The really nice thing is that God doesn't hold our sins over our heads either." That let us both relax.

A word of caution must be given about minimizing the counselees' sins. Do not tell them, "You couldn't help it—it wasn't your fault." If you make statements like this and they believe otherwise you will lose your credibility with them. If you doubt that certain things were their fault ask questions such as "what aspect of this are you holding yourself responsible for and/or what aspects do you blame on the other person?" Let your counselees make the value judgments. It can keep you from looking foolish.

After guilt and blame issues have been clarified I usually restate how I view people and how I try to help people. A common response to counselees is: "I am not as interested in what you have done as I am in helping you decide who you want to be. I believe in change if you want to change, and I am committed to believing in you until you have the strength to believe in yourself. If we stay open and honest with each other I am sure this can happen." These words are usually well taken and often open up the person to new levels of self-exploration.

AREAS OF ASSESSMENT

A number of areas need to be explored as you try to assess your homosexual counselee. Here are some I focus on:

129

1. Family of origin (Mom, Dad, brothers, and sisters)
2. Later family or living experiences (divorce, remarriage, etc.)
3. History of relationship with same-sex parent
4. History of relationship with opposite-sex parent
5. Relationships with brothers and sisters
6. Impressions of parents' affectional and sexual life together
7. History of his or her sexual confusion (When did you first feel different? What was grade school like? Tell me about junior high; tell me about high school. How were you viewing sex by the time you were college age? etc.)
8. Specific history of opposite-sex relationships
9. Specific history of same-sex relationships
10. Detailed account of current sex practices (including fantasy, masturbation, cruising, and sexual relationships)
11. Current views of homosexuality (causality, change possibilities, views of the lifestyle)

I am careful to tell counselees that I will be writing down facts and impressions as we discuss each category and that I will be trying to see how different things fit together. I usually share my view that if we can understand how the behavior was acquired we will probably be able to help them decide what to do about it. I usually don't share a lot of my personal views or biases until the counselee asks. Some counselees are looking for an excuse to turn off the counselor and avoid their problems. I try not to give them that excuse, at least until I know more about their situation.

ASSESSMENT INTERVIEW CONTENT

With these broad assessment categories in mind we can now turn to more specifics about each category.

Family of Origin

Learning about the family of origin is usually a safe place to begin. People know how to tell about their families even though some details may be painful. I use this as an opportunity to get started without having to probe too deeply.

I am particularly sensitive to issues related to adoption or single-parent families because I have found that counselees may have feelings about these circumstances which may need to be discussed at a later point. Sometimes I ask, "Do you think that being adopted (or raised by only one parent) has anything to do with your sexual confusion?" There are no right or wrong answers here—I just want to know what they have thought about and, if possible, what they believe.

Some counselees feel especially guilty over their homosexual struggle if they feel their parent or parents have gone beyond the call of duty for them. Mike said, "How can I do this to them? They didn't have to be my parents. I sure owe them more than this." Assessment of these feelings may have more to do with helping you focus on issues for counseling than with understanding causality. In any regard they should be noted.

Later Family Experience

Very often, breaks in family relationships can change the life of the children drastically. For this reason I feel it is important to understand not only the changes which counselees have encountered but also the meaning those changes can have for them. It is very important to look at the patterns of interaction which resulted from the family breakup. How did the child relate to the father, mother, and new friends of parents or stepparents which may have come on the scene? I am also interested in the messages about masculinity or femininity which may have been given to the counselee at the time the family was breaking up.

Joe said, "I guess I learned that women are to be cared for but never loved. I couldn't stand all the things that men did to my mom and I vowed never to treat women that way." Later, Joe was able to see that this fear of hurting women was a part of the sexual aversion he felt.

In other family situations, children have been introduced to new patterns of sexuality and thus a struggle was begun. One young woman said, "Things were so bad I wanted someone to love me. My stepsister was there and we got into some habits which really got out of hand."

Relationship with the Same-Sex Parent

As was stated in the chapter on causality, Dr. Elizabeth Moberly believes that a breakdown in the relationship with the same-sex parent is an important causal factor in homosexuality. If this is true it is very important to assess your counselees' feelings and beliefs as well as their experiences related to the parent of the same sex. She writes,

From amidst a welter of details, one constant underlying principle suggests itself: that the homosexual—whether man or woman—has suffered from some deficit in the relationship with the parent *of the same sex*; and that there is a corresponding drive to make good this deficit—through the medium of same-sex, or "homosexual," relationships.[1]

There are four major areas I try to assess in relation to the same-sex parent. These are: degree of closeness with the parent, expressions of affection between counselee and the parent, messages received from the parent regarding the child's masculinity or femininity, and covert messages of rejection.

In order to achieve a degree of closeness I ask counselees to talk about pleasant memories they may have shared with me previously, or bad memories, if that is all that seems to be there. I ask about touch and times spent alone together with the parent. Unfortunately, I often hear "Well he/she just never seemed to have time for me." Sometimes this is associated with one specific memory which symbolizes rejection or a lack of attachment. If all the memories seem to be pleasant I do not try to force counselees to come up with bad ones; but my experience has often been that they do this later in the counseling process.

I am especially sensitive to the presence or absence of physical affection. There is a dangerous myth that implies that touching one's child of the same sex or showing affection might make him or her homosexual. I have found that it probably works in reverse. I ask such questions as, "Were you hugged and kissed by your dad (or mom)?" "How did you know when you pleased them?" "How did you handle their displeasure with you?" The affection bonds usually determine who the child

132

identifies with. The child needs to identify with the same-sex parent, but may not if there has not been adequate affection.

I want to know what messages the counselees got from the parent regarding the counselees' success or failure in sex-appropriate behavior. Dennis said, "The message from Dad was always the same. I wasn't adequate. At one point he even said, 'You'll probably grow up to be a homosexual. You can't even throw a ball.'" I ask counselees to try to identify tape recordings which may be playing in their heads from childhood. These recordings often reveal a lot about the things the same-sex parent had to say about his or her child's adequacy. Julie remembered being told over and over again that she was just a tomboy and probably wouldn't ever be a lady.

There are tapes that play in people's heads (covert messages received from parents) and there are messages left by parents which, although covert, tend to leave an indelible impression. Frank said, "Dad never took me fishing. I guess he was afraid I couldn't handle the bait." Sue said, "Why didn't my mother ever dress me up in frilly little dresses like she did my baby sister? I decided dresses and being feminine wasn't right for me."

All persons receive covert messages, not only from same-sex parents but from other family members as well. It is important to take the time to explore these as you assess your counselees.

Relationship with the Opposite-Sex Parent

Although I do not believe the relationship with the opposite-sex parent is as crucial to the homosexual struggle as the one with the same-sex parent, understanding this relationship is very important. I have seen cases in which the relationship with the opposite-sex parent was so bad the counselee could not possibly think of relating sexually to a person of the opposite sex. Pete said, "I hated that witch so bad I could never think of putting a part of my body close to someone like her." Barriers like this must be understood and overcome if any kind of positive relationship is to be developed.

The same four issues which are explored with the same-sex parent—closeness, affection, overt and covert messages—need to be explored in relation to the opposite-sex parent. The more you understand them the more you will understand your counselee.

Relationships with Brothers and Sisters

Sexual behavior is learned and it is often learned by imitation. For this reason it is important to see what kind of behavior may have been learned from your counselees' siblings. Counselees often report that they first learned about sex from a brother or sister. These early experiences have sometimes escalated into sexual patterns or attitudes which may have real bearing on your counselees' behavior.

Larry remembered trying to "do it" with his younger sister. He was too young to know what "it" really was that he was trying to do, but nevertheless he was greatly affected by the experience. His father caught them in an undressed state and told Larry how bad it was to try to do things like that to girls. He even threatened to cut his penis off if he caught him doing such naughty things again. Larry was at such an impressionable age that he developed a fear of sex, particularly with women. We determined this fear to be a causal factor in his homosexual struggle. We would never have discovered it without assessing in detail his relationships with siblings.

Impressions of Parents' Affectional and Sexual Relationship

In growing up as a child I often wondered if my parents ever made love. I knew that they liked each other and I was pretty sure that if they hadn't made love at least once I wouldn't be around, but they were discreet. I was fortunate in that I did grow up thinking that it was possible for a man and a woman to give and receive pleasure from each other. Others have not been so fortunate.

Attitudes are often learned by observation and there is no better way to assess a counselee's attitude than to explore what was observed in the parental relationship. I believe that a person may adopt certain patterns of sexual arousal that he or she has first learned in the home, observing how pleasure was received or not received between the parents. I not only question counselees about their recollections of parental interaction; I often give them an assignment to write down as many things as they can remember between sessions.

Personal History of Sexual Confusion

Where did it all seem to start—is it recent or does it seem to have always been there? Sometimes counselees are asking themselves these questions. During the assessment interview you can guide them through the process of finding some answers for themselves.

I ask counselees to go back as far as their memories will take them. Sometimes this is early childhood—other times it is a later stage in life. The important thing for them is to begin to speak their memories so that they can learn more about themselves. I always ask, "What is your first recollection of feeling that you might not be like everyone else?" Sometimes the answers go back to the choice of toys or wanting to be the opposite sex. At other times, persons relate to junior-high or high-school experiences which began to change their perceptions of self. Regardless, I try to help counselees remember as much as possible about how they felt at different stages of their lives and what experiences they had. For young men I often find that the crisis came during the junior-high or early high-school years. For young women it may be college or later. I usually take this overall history during the first assessment interview and then follow it up in the later interviews with specific questions about their experiences with both males and females. It is usually amazing to discover how much counselees remember once their memories are challenged. The overall history of sexual confusion is a good way to get the process started.

History of Opposite-Sex Relationships

Sometimes this history is very short. There may not be a history. Scott said, "I've never even tried to kiss a girl." Some counselees have even become indignant that I would suggest that they could have had any opposite-sex experience. Usually, however, if I am patient enough the memories will begin to come. The first recollections may not be of sexual experiences at all. Sometimes they are issues of "like or dislike." I work

135

very hard to thoroughly explore this area because if counselees have more experience than that of which they are consciously aware, their views of themselves and their potential for change may be affected.

After the assessment interviews are complete and working hypotheses are formed I will still go back to early experiences to see if anything new has surfaced. This is important because the counselor is often dealing with both repression and selective perception. (Elsewhere I call it "filtering.")

Frank believed for months that his relationship with his fiancée during college days was platonic. As the counseling process got underway he remembered being sexually responsive to her and her being excited about him. These memories later proved to be foundational for change.

Counselors need to be careful to focus on the counselees' attitudes toward events as well as upon the events themselves. The attitudes may have done more to shape the person's perceptions of self than the experiences.

Frank believed that he had been inadequate in his relationship with his fiancée. As he put it, "I just didn't think I had been a man." This caused him to believe that the reason why she was not responsive to him sexually was because something was wrong with him. This led him to view himself as a homosexual even though he did tell me later that his fiancée had been somewhat restrained because of her religious beliefs.

History of Same-Sex Relationships

Experience with the same sex often leads to the development of filters by which the counselees believe or disbelieve that they are homosexual. In assessing this area, counselors need to consider both mental activity as well as overt behavior. I believe strongly that the less overt behavior there has been the greater the possibility of change by the counselee. Sexual activity strengthens fantasies which in turn control future behavior.

Sometimes, early homosexual encounters are very frightening but also alluring for the counselee. Robert reported getting sick at the stomach the first time he got sexually involved with a man. "I went back though," he said, "because I knew I had pleased him." He did go back and the next time he didn't get sick.

As I help counselees try to assess their experiences with the same sex I try to get a feel for the nature of the relationships. Were they coercive or did they do what they did by mutual consent? Were the relationships one-sided? Was the act with friends or strangers? Was it a single incident or were there repeated acts? I am also interested in trying to learn how each experience may have contributed to the counselee's overall views of self.

Other factors to consider in assessing this aspect are the degree of guilt felt, the need to rationalize the behavior, and current aspects of same-sex involvement. Counselors who are straight may have difficulty understanding why such relationships persist. Be careful not to tell your counselees what they should think or feel. Your job, particularly during the assessment phase, is to find out what they actually *do* think or feel.

During this phase of assessment the issue of anonymous versus intimate sex usually comes up. I asked Tim what he was looking for when he went to the shopping mall to make a sexual contact. He said, "Someone I can share my life with." The more we compared this goal with his actual experiences the more we realized that he was not forming social relationships. He was only giving or receiving temporary pleasure. This awareness became a very important counseling issue later on.

Current Sexual Practices

Before you are in a position to help counselees change you need to know how they are currently living. This includes their thought life as well as current relationships. Cindy told me she was afraid she was a lesbian. What I didn't realize until later in the assessment process was that she was living with a woman lover and had been for several months. Edward reported that he masturbated every day and always did so in response to pictures of males. Others reported limited sexual fantasy and no sexual contact. You will not know what is going on with your counselees until you assess this area. Sometimes counselees will withhold important information from you, but usually, as your relationship with them grows, they will become more honest.

When I apologized for what therapy was costing Lewis he said, "Don't worry—you're saving me money and probably saving my life." He reported that prior to seeing me he had been cruising either mentally or in his car as much as eighty hours per week. This late bit of assessment information was used in setting a goal of not cruising at all in his car and cutting in half the amount of time in fantasy related to sexual contact with males. As this goal was reached some of the other more important issues could be dealt with.

As a counselor you need to find out what is going on and you also need periodically to check to see what changes are actually taking place. If you hear lots of talk about need to change but see no behavioral change, something is wrong and you need to discuss the issue with your counselee.

Current Views of Homosexuality

Routinely, as part of the assessment process, I ask my counselees to share their views about themselves and their struggle with same-sex preference. This time is very important because it will help me to know what limits the counselees may be putting on the counseling process. I ask about lifestyle and ask them to project themselves into the future. I also inquire about their views of change and what change will require of them. The issue of causality is also approached from the counselees' perspective because it helps me to know what influences other than counseling they have encountered. Duke said, "I believe I can change—sorta—but I'm the only one of my friends who believes that." If Duke is to change, the issue of competing influences is one he will have to face.

During the discussion of current views of homosexuality I try to find out about counselees' fears, such as AIDS or of becoming old and ugly. (This is a common fear among male homosexuals.) I have found that these fears often have a large bearing on their motivation to continue in counseling.

Lastly, I try to assess the counselees' views of God and try to determine if for them God is a possible resource in their struggle with homosexuality. I usually ask the question,

"Some of my counselees are religious or have a personal faith. Do you see this as a resource for you personally?" If the counselee affirms a personal faith I may share my belief that God is indeed ready and willing to help. If the counselee does not appear to have a personal faith I will often say, "I have a personal faith which is very meaningful to me. I don't think that will get in the way of our relationship, but if you want to ask me more about it or are confused by something I might say in this regard, do not hesitate to ask." On more than one occasion counselees have asked and I have shared how I see God as relevant to human problems. I usually do this on my time, not theirs.

Information Gathering—Then What?

Once information is being gathered, you as the counselor are faced with the task of making sense out of it and then using it with the counselee. There are several steps I go through that help me in this process.

1. I keep a written list of hypotheses related to causality. As stated earlier, I believe that if I understand how counselees got where they are I am then in a better position to help them get from there to where they say they want to be. If I know how the behavior was learned I can better help them unlearn it.

2. As I gain information which might serve to confirm or disconfirm each hypothesis, I make note of it.

3. Periodically, I give counselees an update on what I am thinking and ask them to tell me if it makes any sense to them. Usually, if I have not come across as too authoritarian, my counselees are very open to say they agree or disagree. If they agree, we proceed cautiously. If they disagree, we look for other possible explanations.

4. As I go through the assessment process with the counselee I keep a list of issues to be explored. Later I will come back to this list and ask the counselee to indicate which ones he or she feels need to be discussed. Sometimes the issues relate specifically to the homosexual struggle. At other times they may be more related to self-esteem or nonsexual aspects of relationships. I usually try to focus first on the issues that seem to be the biggest for the counselee.

5. After the topic of causality has been addressed and other issues outlined, I usually move to goal-setting. I need to reach agreement with the counselee on what we are seeking to accomplish. I always encourage small, reachable goals.

6. I usually explain that with the goals we have a starting place. Some of our starts will be quite successful and the goals may be reached quickly. On the other hand, I explain that the assessment process is never over and as we go through the counseling process we will come up with new memories, new perceptions, new concerns, and new goals. I tell them that when this happens we will clarify where we are and keep moving onward.

7. I regularly reassure my counselees that what they tell me is confidential and that I will not use it as the topic of casual conversation. I do, however, reserve one right. I ask counselees for permission to seek consultation from other professionals if I feel a need to do so. I assure them that if I should do this I will not use their names or give out data that could result in a violation of their confidence. Most counselees have been extremely cooperative in this regard.

Assessment, especially the assessment interview, is the heart of successful counseling with homosexuality. Do it carefully and thoroughly, keeping in mind it is a dynamic process that is never complete.

CHAPTER NINE

HELPFUL MODELS: VERBAL AND VISUAL

BECAUSE COUNSELING IS SUCH A SPECIALIZED COMMUNICATION PROCESS it requires that we use all our creative energies in order to be effective. We must be very conscious of how our counselees learn, and concentrate our communication efforts in such a way as to take advantage of their individual learning styles. Some people retain best what they hear while others learn more rapidly when the concepts can be presented to them in some visual fashion. Regarding the understanding of learning styles or learning channels, Welter writes:

One way to understand the concept of learning channels is to imagine that you live in a TV viewing area where you

141

are able to get three channels, only one of which gives you good reception. A second channel is fair, although the fidelity may be poor and it may have some "snow." Let's suppose that the third channel is very weak. You have to work hard just to get the main idea of a given program on that channel. This is somewhat like learning channels, because often one may be strong and another weak.[1]

Although Welter presents three learning channels (verbal, visual, and haptic-motor), we will concentrate on presenting models for communication which are based on the first two—verbal and visual—which are the most commonly used.

DEVELOPING VERBAL MODELS

Words can be very powerful and life changing, or they can be confusing and dull. There is nothing automatic about communication. The power is in the choice and presentation of words. Words may bring you and your counselees closer to each other and closer to truth and understanding, or they may establish barriers which inhibit both relationship and understanding. All counselors need to heed the truth contained in the following excerpt from *The Little Prince*.

"One only understands the things that one tames," said the fox to the little prince, who was in search of a friend.
"If you want a friend, tame me."
"What must I do, to tame you?" asked the little prince.
"You must be very patient," replied the fox.
"First you will sit down at a little distance from me—like that—in the grass. I shall look at you out of the corner of my eye, and you will say nothing. Words are the source of misunderstanding. But you will sit a little closer to me, every day."[2]

This quotation is itself a verbal model. It provides a word picture of a process of developing friendship that is not so different from counseling. If you are communicating with your counselees you will notice them becoming more involved. They will lean toward you, they will nod their heads, and they will elaborate more on questions you ask. If they do not understand, their words will become fewer and fewer and you as a counselor will become more frustrated. If you see that this has happened with a particular counselee you may need to sharpen your verbal models or use more visuals. Here are some guidelines which I try to follow in creating word pictures (visual models) for counselees.

Guidelines for Developing Verbal Models

1. Use the words that are most familiar to the counselees. Watch for words that they often repeat. Make sure you understand how they use those words. Build your communication around those words.

2. Do not use technical words unless it is absolutely necessary. When you do use technical words or jargon have your counselees explain the jargon to you in their own words. For example, I often use the term *obsessional thought* with homosexual counselees. I need to make sure they understand.

After some discussion, Marvin, a counselee, and I decided that my technical phrase, "obsessional thought," when translated into his words, was "the tapes that keep playing in my head." He understood this concept because the words were his. I was glad to change my words to accommodate him because I wanted to communicate.

3. Use words that describe action and people and circumstances. Counselors are usually too abstract.

I asked Marvin how loud the tapes were playing. I also asked him how many hours per day they played. The answers to these questions provided me with needed understanding about the intensity and the pervasiveness of his sexual obsession. Later in the counseling process it was helpful to use the verbal models of "turning down the volume" or "turning off the machine." These two word pictures were useful tools in his learning to control his sexual obsession.

4. Paint verbal pictures that coincide with the counselee's background. If your counselee understands sports, use analogies from sports. If the counselee has interests in fashion, use illustrations from that area. Always concentrate upon the best-known areas and venture into the unknown only when

necessary. We have a misconception that good communication and counseling teach people things they did not previously know. I believe that good counseling must start by clarifying what is known and incorporating new insights into the most basic understandings.

To continue the example of Marvin and the tape that plays in his head, I did not find it useful to explain the technical aspects of obsessional thought in order to help him change. What was helpful, however, was to go to something he understood quite well.

"Marvin," I asked, "what happens when you are listening to the radio and a friend begins to talk to you?"

"I can't concentrate," he replied. "Pretty soon I have to stop listening or talking."

I used this to help him see that introducing other verbal input can be helpful in undermining the strength of the obsession. As a result of this he started listening to music or talking to friends more often instead of just letting the tape run without any competition.

5. Finally, test out your verbal models from time to time to see if counselees are still using them. Ask about the tape recorder. Ask how the volume is. Ask about the frequency of the tape playing. I have often found that as counselees progress in counseling they will develop their own new models which replace the old ones and which represent the changes that have occurred.

Marvin said, "You know, it isn't a tape anymore. It is more like a radio signal that interferes once in a while. It is still there, but it isn't very loud and it doesn't always bother me." This insight was helpful to Marvin as a means of revealing the progress he had made and it was helpful to me in formulating new verbal models to help him screen out the unwanted radio signal.

Creating Verbal Models with Your Counselees

Whenever possible, solicit your counselees' help in sharpening the communication process. Ask what certain words and phrases bring to their minds. Then use the words that seem to have the most power.

I like to pick up on examples or experiences which counselees share and then use them to help focus attention on a given area. In essence I am creating verbal models with the counselee.

Tom was a student in business administration at the university, so he knew a lot about taking tests. I helped him broaden this concept and to think of the "test" of self-control as we sought to help him become free of his habit of casual sexual contact. I would ask: Have you taken any tests this week? What are you doing to get ready for the test? He knew what I meant and was able to approach his problem better when he saw it as a test. Others may have been turned off by this model but for Tom it was a source of motivation and an instant communicator.

Sometimes counselees will pick up on words or phrases which I use that are not familiar to them. Their new awareness of the use of a word may be very helpful in developing communication together. Ruth said, "What was that phrase you used a while ago? I don't think I have ever thought of it before." After a little effort I realized I had talked about people's ability to self-destruct. I explained what I had meant and she identified with the idea. We had a new verbal model that we could use together. I later learned that she translated her word pictures into a visual model or picture and that she had formed this mental image: Unhealthy sexual conduct leads to her fainting and being left to die. This certainly wasn't the image I would use, but for her it was very useful and as long as I could identify with it we did well.

Everett Worthington uses a verbal model in the form of a fable to help counselees with loneliness.[3] I have used a similar technique in which I tell counselees a story and ask if they see any similarity between my story and their lives. Usually, if I have put proper thought into it, the counselees will readily identify with the points I am trying to make.

If your counselees use words with ease and are verbally comfortable, then taking advantage of their ability to create verbal models will greatly enhance the counseling relationship.

USING VISUAL MODELS

Some counselees think in pictures and will only become more confused unless the words you use can be translated into pictures. I asked Martha to explain to me what I had just said. She took my meager words and transformed them into a beautiful picture. She had literally "seen" what I was saying. After I realized this about her I worked harder to use picture words with her. Instead of telling her stories, which is my usual style, I would describe scenes. It helped our communication greatly.

I have counseled with many male homosexuals who are very visual; they enjoy art and they think in pictures. This is foreign to some men who are either touch oriented or verbal. I believe counselors do a better job with visual counselees once they see how the counselees view the world.

George said, "I can still see the disappointment carved on my dad's face." At that point I resisted the urge to ask, "what did he say?" (a verbal response) and asked instead, "can you describe it more?" Then I asked, "What else can you see engraved there?" This opened the door for him to share many more emotions he had felt in relationship with his father. They were emotions painted like a great mural across his memory.

Guidelines for Developing Visual Models

There are several steps you can follow in developing visual models with your counselees.

1. Pay special attention to statements that reveal a visual orientation. Words like "I see" or "it looks like" are good cues. Ask direct questions such as "would you rather talk, or look at pictures?" "Which way do you think you learn best?"

2. When you ascertain that your counselees are visually oriented take full advantage of the opportunity to have them describe events and situations in which they may have experienced a lot of emotion.

I asked Joan to describe a scene that best described her relationship with her mother. Her memory for details in terms of what she was wearing and where she was sitting revealed a great deal about the importance of the situation and the various emotions she had experienced. She couldn't say she was sad (verbal), but she could picture the tears running down her cheeks.

3. Ask your counselees to describe situations they would like to experience. If they are visual ask them to describe the

type of home they want for themselves. Don't ask them to tell you what they want out of life.

4. Finally, have counselees describe scenes that will reveal their views of change or progress. Some may even be asked to draw cartoon-type pictures which show their progress over time. Let your counselees work on these for homework and bring them in to you. This will facilitate their growth and self-understanding.

BE AWARE OR BE FRUSTRATED

Even when the most helpful models of communication are selected and used, counselees respond in different ways and at their own pace. Don't be discouraged when you may not be getting through as well as you would like. When you are dealing with homosexuality you are dealing with a counselee who is in a severe struggle. Any new concepts you communicate will take time to be integrated. As a counselor you need to be aware of the up-and-down feelings your counselee is going through so that you will not be frustrated or lose confidence in yourself or your counselee. Sometimes it is difficult to determine whether your counselee is not making progress because you have not communicated, or because the communication received by the counselee is too heavy to deal with at the moment. Don't change models unless you determine that the problem is *in the communication* and not in the response to the communication.

Ralph said, "When I first began to get hold of the things you were telling me I really felt overwhelmed. At times I wanted to shout, 'Leave me alone, I can't deal with this!'" Ralph struggled for weeks. He tried to deal with all the side issues without getting back to the major areas. He became more despondent, even to the point of wanting to commit suicide. After a half-hearted attempt at overdosing he said, "I never intended to take my life. I guess I was just making a statement about how hard all this is for me."

At that point I asked Ralph to make the statement on paper. I wanted to capitalize on his verbal ability in order to help him begin to grow. He wrote what he was feeling and in the process his feelings began to be more accessible to him. He realized that he had not been willing to change because of his fear of losing all his friends. Once this feeling was out, so that it could be dealt with, the growth process was begun.

Kell and Mueller have written about how underlying feelings from the past, which they call "compacted," can hinder growth and even affect the counselor-counselee relationship.

> The client risks expanding some of the feelings associated with his compacted experiences as the counseling relationship matures and becomes more and more significant to him. The client's willingness to risk the anxiety of expanding these experiences is in part a function of how effectively the counselor has touched on the general affective theme of the client's compacted experiences.[4]

As feelings begin to expand for the counselee he or she may become fearful. Understanding feelings may bring healing but it may also foster resistance to counseling. If the counseling relationship is strong the resistance may pass; if it is weak the counselee may even drop out of counseling.

We can see that when emotions from the past are brought into current needs and expectations, the process of getting started may be slow. Selecting good counseling models helps, but growth will still be erratic. In this kind of situation it is easy for the counselor to get overinvested in "helping the counselee to change"; your worth gets tied into being a "competent" counselor. I believe in striving for excellence, but I also know that we must be realistic about what we can and cannot do for our counselees.

There are situations in which I have become so concerned about helping that I have pushed too hard or listened too little, which resulted in a breakdown in the counseling relationship. I wanted so much to be competent that I became incompetent.

The counselee may also seek to immobilize you in order to keep from changing. The more skilled you are the more the counselee may resist your skills or fight your efforts toward progress. Kell and Mueller refer to this as the double-edged sword of being adequate. They write,

Adequacy is the counselor's passport to unraveling his client's conflicts and effecting change. But adequacy is a double-edged sword and it can easily shade into omnipotence on the one hand and impotence on the other hand. The counselor's adequacy will most assuredly activate the client's conflicts, and the client's conflicted feelings in turn will trigger a wish to immobilize the counselor in order to keep from changing. Since the client's present situation, although discomforting, is more comfortable than the prospect of exploring the unknown, he will become hypersensitive to chinks in the armor of the counselor's adequacy. In this respect, the counselor's adequacy makes him vulnerable to attack as the client searches for ways of maintaining his old emotional state and attempts to keep from changing.[5]

It is important that you as a counselor be aware enough of your own skills so that you can patiently work through the growth struggles your counselee is experiencing.

"Ralph," I said, "I want you to make progress and I believe we are on the right track, but it doesn't look like I can bite the bullet for you. Change is out there but you are the one who has to go for it."

COGNITIVE VS. AFFECTIVE UNDERSTANDING

Just as counselees have different learning channels there are also different levels of learning which must be reached before behavioral change can occur.

Many Christians are very cognitively oriented. We believe in truth and we believe that truth can change people. We are sometimes shocked, however, when we realize that people know what is right and may even know what they have to do but are not taking any steps forward. Their intellect is where it needs to be, but their emotions are not. One reason for this is that cognitive and emotional learning take place differently and at different rates of speed. In fact, the learning takes place in different parts of the brain. If we keep this in mind we will stop trying to convince people to change their emotions based on cognitive arguments. Emotional change is usually brought about by experience, not argumentation.

One of my counselees could recite all of the reasons why he should stay out of leather bars (drinking establishments where various homosexual rituals associated with leather are conducted). He kept going, however, until one night when he was tied up with leather and his body was shaved. The humiliation he experienced was enough for emotional learning to occur.

Not all counselees have to go through humiliation in order for emotional learning to occur. Visual or verbal models can be created which can help them learn without going through negative experiences. Visual imagery such as that practiced by some of those skilled in directing inner healing can be very valuable.[6]

I used verbal imagery with a counselee, Nick, who was trying to stop homosexual contact. I had him repeat what his son or daughter might say if they caught him in the act. The thought of words from his son asking, "Daddy, what are you and that man doing with your underwear down?" was adequate to facilitate emotional learning to go along with the cognitive belief that he had to stop.

Emotional learning is one component of what we call *attitudes*. Gagne has written concerning the nature of attitude change,

> Many of our attitudes are learned as a result of a series of interactions with other people—with parents, friends, and associates. Attitudes may be acquired or changed rather suddenly as the result of a single experience. Or they may undergo gradual change over a period of years, presumably as the result of a cumulative series of experiences.[7]

As a counselor who wants to promote attitude change and emotional growth, you will be wise to use as many different models and experiences as you can think of in order to stimulate change in your counselee. You never quite know what will be the most helpful; but try as many different approaches as you can think of. Careful planning will help you to move your counselee from cognitive learning, which is the basis for change, to emotional learning, which is the key to change.

That purely intellectual understanding unaccompanied by a corrective emotional experience in relationship to another person is often ineffective is illustrated by the intelligent, introspective client. Such clients are often highly accurate, as later events often prove, about the nature of their problems and even about the origins of their difficulties. Yet these clients still speak of themselves as deeply dissatisfied with the changes they have made and with the rewards that accrue to them from the external world. The same clients, after an emotionally disrupting experience such as counseling may be, will report with conviction years later that their lives have changed for the better.[8]

Working with Obsessions

All counseling involves working with obsessions, but this is paramount in counseling with homosexuality. Wolpe defines obsessions as "recurrent, persistent ideas or impulses."[9] Many homosexuals are so preoccupied with sexual thoughts or thoughts about their "problem" that they have difficulty thinking about anything else.

Ed confessed, "If you define worship as what I think about the most, I must worship sex. It seems to be all I think about these days."

Cammer writes,

Many obsessions focus on sex. Unlike stimulating sensual fantasies, these obsessions are usually repugnant. A prudish girl pictures vivid scenes of "kinky" sexual behavior in revolting postures; a decorous businessman cannot rid himself of desires to take part in "perverted" sexual acts involving several partners, some animals; or an adolescent must fight off the urge to masturbate in public.

You were the formal, elderly woman who complained that "dirty" words and phrases kept invading your mind. To boot, all the words seemed to go with rape: undrape, dilate, ejaculate, masturbate, violate. In a similar predicament a professor of history is plagued by "sexual limericks that are always filthy" with homosexual overtones. When he tries to rid himself of such thoughts, equally dirty rhymes replace them.[10]

I believe that Scripture has some very helpful suggestions regarding the importance of controlling the mind if one is to control the behavior.

Finally, brethren, whatsoever things are true, whatsoever things are honest, whatsoever things are just, whatsoever things are pure, whatsoever things are lovely, whatsoever things are of good report; if there be any virtue, and if there be any praise, think on these things. (Phil. 4:8 KJV)

For as he thinketh in his heart, so is he. (Prov. 23:7a KJV)

Thought control can be approached from both a Christian (scriptural) orientation, or from a behavioral (mind control) approach. I have found the two approaches quite compatible.

Will's mind was flooded by visual images of men's bodies. He couldn't seem to stop it. I suggested that he quote Scripture aloud when he was overwhelmed. This helped. He couldn't think of the Scripture and the visual image at the same time. Tom discovered a similar technique for himself. He realized he couldn't act on his lustful thoughts and listen to praise tapes at the same time. Betty prayed when she felt an obsession taking over. As she concentrated on what she wanted to say to God the thoughts of her lover were extinguished.

Behavioral psychologists have taught thought stopping for years. A technique I use is to ask my counselee to wear a rubber band loosely on his or her arm. When obsessions start they are to flip themselves with the band and then change their thoughts to something nonsexual. You may have to help counselees pre-select some positive topics to which they can turn. Arm them with a list to which they can readily turn. Something relaxing or pleasant is helpful; flowers or football or a memory of a quiet walk in the forest may be helpful. Cammer stresses the value of thought stopping. He writes,

With behavior therapy you can reestablish personal mind control for your actions, feelings or thoughts (a control you lost when you became maladaptive). We know that, pragmatically, maladaptive behavior may be stopped, redirected, reinforced or modified in many ways. Paralleling this, the anxiety-vigilance-fear-anger complex of uptightness can also be conditioned and altered for emotional control. Thought stopping is one of the techniques in behavior therapy for ideational control. It is a strong influence in eliminating or reducing the distress of obsessions, ruminations and doubts.[11]

Relaxation is also a helpful tool in dealing with obsessions. Some obsessions are brought on by anxiety and can be stopped if the person can learn to relax. Unfortunately, many persons who are anxious have learned to use masturbation or sexual obsession to relax. In such cases the obsession will be harder to stop because it is maintained by both the relaxation and the positive reinforcement of sexual pleasure. Obsessional behavior maintains itself. Once the anxiety is lessened or adapted to by the person, other reinforcers such as pleasure keep the obsession alive.

Anxiety or body tension is often the cue counselees read that starts them down the obsessional path. The anxiety is the first link in the chain. If you can help your counselees learn to relax the chain will be broken before it becomes destructive.

Don't take for granted your counselees' ability to relax. If they knew how, they would probably have been doing it all along. Provide them with some books or tapes that will help them learn; and give them time during the counseling session to practice what they are learning.[12]

In general, obsessions are best overcome by starvation. When a person stops feeding them they die. This means that if a counselee who is very visual stops looking at pictures of nude males the obsession with nude males will weaken. As counselees stop practicing homosexuality the obsession often weakens. Prolonged abstinence has great value. The key is to help the person realize the importance of stopping the obsession.

As long as he or she remains attached to the obsession no change will occur. Thought stopping begins when the counselee agrees that continuing the thought pattern is futile and needs to be eliminated.

Aversive Conditioning

Behavioral psychologists have historically treated obsessions and homosexuality with aversive conditioning. This has usually taken the form of a low level electric shock being administered to the counselee during the obsession or after a stimulus has been presented that might evoke homosexual thoughts. This procedure is quite controversial and needs to be addressed here.

The objections raised range from the contention that the procedure is inhumane to the belief that it doesn't work. Both of these objections are at least partially true. Although administering low level shock is not harmful to the counselee it may be dehumanizing and should not be used except in those cases where the counselee is in full agreement. When I use any procedure that involves punishment I prefer that the punishment be self-administered. I would only use aversive conditioning when the obsessions are so strong that they preclude other forms of treatment. In such cases, the use of aversive conditioning for a brief time so that obsessions can be controlled and other therapy implemented could be justified with counselee consent.

The objection that aversive conditioning doesn't work is not true as stated. Punishment will suppress responses and it will do so in a short period of time. But it is not effective in eliminating the behavior. It only suppresses it. Through self-administration of a nauseous-smelling substance John was able to bring his obsession under control. After two weeks he was advised to stop the self-punishment but continue to come for therapy which was designed to teach thought control. He felt so good about his progress that he stopped counseling altogether. After only three weeks he was right back where he had started. When punishment is removed the undesired behavior will return.

Turner, Calhoun, and Adams discuss the elimination of deviant arousal.

Although a sexually deviant individual may regard his sexual activity as repugnant and may actually desire alteration of his sexual orientation, his deviant sexual behavior has acquired reinforcing properties by virtue of its connection with orgasmic pleasure. It should be noted that aversion therapy is designed to eliminate undesirable responses but does not ensure the development of alternative, desirable behaviors. As we have indicated earlier, eliminating an undesirable sexual response is not sufficient unless the patient has learned alternative, appropriate means of gratifying sexual urges. Thus the effectiveness of aversion therapy is enhanced when there is training for the patient in a satisfactory, alternative form of sexual arousal and behavior.[13]

The use of aversive conditioning should not be undertaken without consultation with a trained mental health professional who has experience with this method. It may be helpful in some cases but must be carefully thought out before it is used.

Counseling is first and foremost good communication. In this chapter we have presented some models which can help you to communicate better with your counselees who are struggling with homosexuality. We have also discussed the growth process and the importance of fostering emotional as well as cognitive learning. Finally, the topic of aversive conditioning has been addressed. It has limitations and should only be used under special conditions when professional consultation and supervision are available.

CHAPTER TEN

TRANSFERENCE, COUNTERTRANSFERENCE, AND OTHER KEY ISSUES

SHORTLY AFTER I BEGAN TO COUNSEL more homosexual counselees I received an obscene telephone call in the middle of the night. As gross and disgusting as it was, it accomplished two useful things for me. First, it made me appreciate the fear and humiliation that many women go through daily. It is terrifying to have an anonymous person talk about using your body as though it belonged to him or her. Second, the telephone call forced me to begin to think about some of my attitudes and behaviors toward my homosexual counselees. I had never really faced questions such as: "How close do I dare get?" or "what will I do if one of my counselees falls in love with me?" or "what if I am attracted to one of my counselees?"

I had always considered that working through these questions was basic to counseling with opposite-sex clients, but had never really considered the impact of working with the same sex. I had been very secure in my heterosexuality and had not worried about many of the issues that arise in dealing with homosexuality. The telephone call had challenged me in some very healthy ways.

COUNSELOR SELF-AWARENESS

As a counselor educator and trainer for over twenty years I have repeatedly preached the necessity for counselors to know themselves. Counseling is a very emotional task and all counselors need to develop their awareness of their emotions. Gary Collins writes,

Counseling is not a step-by-step process such as baking a cake, or changing a tire, or even preparing a sermon. Each counselee is unique—with problems, attitudes, values, expectations, and experiences that are unlike any other. The counselor (whose own problems, attitudes, values, expectations, and experiences are also brought to the counseling situations) must approach each individual a little differently and will discover that the course of counseling will vary from person to person.[1]

A very real part of counselors' "problems, attitudes, values, expectations, and experiences" which are brought into the counseling session has to do with the counselor's awareness of his or her own sexuality. Comfort in this area will be transmitted to the counselee while uncertainty will also be communicated. Fears will be perceived by your counselees. Insecurity and the quality of being judgmental will be read like a book. Counselors, like their counselees, must become aware of their emotions so they can make good choices about their interaction with counselees.

George, one of my students, had asked me to observe a session with one of his counseling practicum counselees. He secured the counselee's permission and I watched from behind the one-way mirror. The counselee was very open and willing to talk. He shared many of his feelings, but somehow George wasn't able to help him get to the issues. The session was amicable, but not very productive. As time went by I could see that George was more and more nervous and uptight. During the briefing that followed, George could not explain his behavior during the session.

"I just don't know what was wrong with me," he said.

"George," I replied, "you seemed to be afraid of getting too close. In fact, when it appeared as though your counselee might tell you his problem was homosexuality, you seemed to change the subject real fast. Were you afraid of what he might tell you?" After some thought George said, "Maybe so!" We talked about his fears for a while and then I decided to open up things even more.

"George," I said, "I have a suspicion that even though you have worked with homosexual clients before, this one is particularly difficult." He nodded and I said, "Perhaps this one is too close for comfort. Maybe you like him too much and are having trouble understanding your feelings."

This was a lot for George to handle, but the more we talked the more my ideas made sense to him. Finally he said, "I don't know what to do. I've never felt this way before."

"What would you do if it were a female counselee?" I asked.

"Just watch myself," he replied. "I'd be careful not to do anything foolish."

"Well," I said, "that's not bad advice for this situation either."

George was quite relieved to have his feelings out in the open and we shared a confidence that the counseling session could get back on track. When feelings are left unidentified the counselor will not be able to act responsibly toward them. When they are identified and counselor ownership of them is taken then good decisions can occur.

I recommended to George that during the next session he allow the counselee to talk about his sexual feelings and sexual preference if that turned out to be the problem. George was able to do this and, interestingly enough, when George actually addressed the issue with the counselee he found his own sexual feelings disappearing.

Other counselors have reported similar feelings about opposite-sex counselees who have sexual problems. Once they talk and the counselor listens, the allurement may not be nearly as great. Lack of awareness can create a fantasy with which the counselor may not be prepared to deal. Openness with self and openness with the counselee will help to keep things in perspective. On the other hand, hiding from one's own emotions may create havoc.

The Counselor's Sexuality

Whenever two people work closely together towards a common goal, feelings of camaraderie and warmth often arise between them. When these people are of similar background, and especially when they are of the opposite sex, the feelings of warmth almost always have a sexual component. This sexual attraction between counselor and counselee has been called "the problem clergymen don't talk about." But it is a problem that almost *all* counselors encounter, at times, whether or not they talk about it with others.[2]

An important part of counselor self-awareness is to realize that one feeling or one encounter does not mean anything by itself. As Collins pointed out, when people talk intimately they are going to experience "feelings of warmth." These feelings of warmth could get interpreted as sexual attraction. Unless you are aware that such happenings could occur you might become confused for nothing. As a general rule, when you become aware of feelings you don't understand there are two courses of action to take. First, go slow, don't make any assumptions, and watch to see where the feelings end up. Second, talk to a confidant who may be able to help you understand yourself better. Sometimes the second step is not necessary if you have followed the first carefully. George, mentioned earlier, needed my insights in order to understand his feelings. His willingness to seek help saved him from continued confusion and mistakes.

UNDERSTAND YOUR COUNSELEES' FEELINGS
TOWARD YOU

Counselors will experience many feelings directed toward them just as they experience many feelings internally. While working with counselees who are struggling with same-sex preference I have sensed suspicion, anger, fear, admiration, love, mistrust, and a yearning for friendship. Although some of these feelings are contradictory your counselee may feel them about you even in the same session.

One client said, "I hate you and yet I want to be close to you because I sense strength and hope." Counselee fear may be related to a fear of being rejected by the counselor or in some cases by a fear of acceptance if one is attracted sexually. In general, you can expect that your counselee will experience a myriad feelings, many of which may be related to you personally. Without trying to cover all the possible situations that might arise I want to concentrate on several emotional situations.

Suspicion or Fear of Counselor Motives

Think for a moment what it is like to be a counselee. You have kept a secret for a long time only to find yourself talking to a stranger whose value system you may not know or understand. You may not even know how to ask the questions that will help you understand your counselor better. The situation is even more complicated if you do not trust authority figures or have had trouble relating to one or more of your parents.

Sarah said, "I knew I didn't like my dad very much so that didn't get you off to a very good start."

Counselees sometimes don't know what to expect from you, particularly as it comes to your expectations that they will change. Paul was upfront with his hostility. "I'm here to get to know you," he said, "but I'll warn you—if you lean on me too much I'll run. I don't know whether you are a shrink or a preacher but I don't trust either."

I thanked Paul for his honesty and said I wanted to concentrate on the two of us getting acquainted so that we would both know what to expect. I assured him that he could ask as many questions as he wanted and I would try to answer them for him. I also took the opportunity to talk about my views of counseling and counselee change.

"Paul," I said, "I don't know how you see me but I'm just here to help you get where you decide to go. I can't make you do anything you don't decide to do, but I have been fairly successful at helping people find ways to reach the goals they have set."

Suspicion and fear of counselor motives are best dealt with by the counselor's recognizing counselees' feelings and giving them permission to feel whatever they are feeling. Openness on the part of the counselor is most useful. Defensiveness on the part of the counselor usually results in greater suspicion and often in a breakdown in the counseling relationship.

Ambivalence and Distancing

Counselees often go up and down in their feelings. Millie was excited and hopeful one day only to be down and gloom-filled during the next counseling session. The counselor discovered that this ambivalence affected the way Millie related to her. She would withdraw verbally during her "down" times, and she even held back after a while when she was up. She was afraid to commit herself for fear she would not be able to follow through, and she withdrew from her counselor because she did not "want to let her down." The counselor realized what was going on and confronted it kindly but directly.

"Millie," she said, "you put yourself through a lot sometimes."

"What do you mean?" Millie replied. The counselor took advantage of the opening.

"I'll tell you what I think and you tell me how it sounds to you. You really have high standards. You would like to be the best at everything and that includes being a really good counselee. How am I doing so far?"

Millie smiled and said, "Pretty much on target." The counselor continued.

"You think I have pretty high standards for you and you want to fix your life up for me, if not for yourself." Millie nodded.

"Here is where the trouble starts," the counselor remarked. "You want to please me and yourself but when you fear that you won't, you get afraid and pull back. You are so afraid of your own ups and downs that you get afraid of me and of counseling for fear of failure. When you pull back you feel safer because at least you can tell yourself that you failed (if you should fail) because you didn't try."

Millie seemed relieved to be able to discuss what was going on. The important thing was not what the counselor said but the fact that she had courage enough to confront the distance she was feeling from Millie. Once the problem was brought out in the open, either one could bring it up and they could work on it together. This openness enabled the counselor to challenge Millie to work on goals again without the pressure of counselor rejection if failure should occur.

Ambivalence and distancing are common feelings for counselees, especially when they feel uncertain of their own feelings or of the counselor's expectations. The best thing the counselor can do is confront the distance and clarify the need for the counselee to work on small, reachable goals. Millie's counselor told her, "Let's work together. I think we can make some good things happen for you." This relieved a lot of the pressure Millie was feeling.

Affection and Love

Because of the social stigma that is attached to homosexuality and lesbianism, many counselors are afraid to react to their gay counselees as they might other counselees. There is an uneasiness when it comes to dealing with expressions of love or affection which might occur.

As Kevin was pouring out his heart to me and I was listening intently I could feel his admiration and affection for me growing. His life up to this point had been very difficult and I was probably the first person who had cared enough to listen. Listening can be very seductive and Kevin was attracted to a man who would hear his pain and even shed a tear. I was not surprised by what was happening with Kevin because I had experienced growing, positive feelings from counselees before. I realized, however, that I had a real responsibility to him not to let my feelings get in the way of productive counseling. At least four things could have happened.

First, I might have communicated to Kevin, either verbally or nonverbally, that his emotion and behavior were out of line. He would have taken this as rejection and he would have ceased to explore his problem, probably forever. Kevin needed to feel affection toward me and he needed to feel affection coming back from me. The key issue is the nature of the expression of affection. When love is right it doesn't have to be sensual to be satisfying.

Second, I might have made the mistake of allowing Kevin to express his affection or love in a sexual way. Just as I would not knowingly hug a heterosexual counselee who is attracted to me I would exercise the same precaution with a counselee of the same sex. One of Kevin's greatest needs was to discover that love and affection for a person of the same sex is possible and that acceptance in such relationships can be experienced nonsexually. Moberly's words are very instructive at this point.

> The homosexual is not to stop loving members of the same sex, but to meet his or her psychological needs deeply and completely without sexual activity. The same-sex relationship is to be so fulfilling that same-sex deficits remain no longer and the relationship itself is outgrown. It may be difficult at first for some Christians to accept that same-sex needs should be fulfilled, but this is necessary and it does not imply sexual activity. One will do well to remember that the capacity for same-sex love is essentially the love-need of the child for the parent, even if not consciously experienced as such. The homoemotional drive thus seeks the fulfillment of this aspect of family life, and it is right and good that Christians should help toward this fulfillment. To do this is, in a special sense, to offer a home to the homeless (Isaiah 58:7), as God himself is said to do (Psalm 68:6).[3]

Third, I might reject the counselee. Sometimes counselors become fearful when positive emotions are expressed and push the counselee away. This only serves to reinforce many of the feelings the counselee may have experienced as a child. As a counselor you do not have to love your counselee, but your behavior does need to be loving and express respect. I find it helpful to recognize that my emotions do not have to match those of my counselees. They can love me more than I love them. We are such romantics that even in counseling we tend to ask the question, "Do you love me as much as I love you?" Such a question is unnecessary and will be counterproductive if not destructive. Do not reject your counselee for loving you, but on the other hand do not feel that you have to match feelings. Just learn to deal with what you do find there emotionally.

The fourth error which might have occurred is what I call the error of untimely exploration. As long as Kevin was continuing to explore his feelings—what I considered healthy exploration of them—there was no need to sidetrack the counseling process by forcing an untimely discussion of the feelings he was having for me. I chose to allow the feelings of affection to be there in an unexplored way until he discovered them and brought them up or until I felt they needed to be addressed if Kevin was to avoid a new level of confusion. I prefer that counseling resolve confusion, not feed it.

During a lull in an interview I said, "Let's talk about some of the feelings we have toward our counseling and toward each other." He looked shocked at first but then, as we began to explore the area, he became noticeably relieved. I told Kevin that I cared for him and that I didn't want anything to hurt the process of counseling. He expressed how close he felt to me and how scary that was for him. He said, "I've never been close to a man before without it leading to sex." I assured him that that would not happen and also told him that I hoped he would benefit greatly from being in a relationship with a man that was safe for him. In essence I was saying, "I care for you too much to get involved at a level that would be destructive for both of us."

As the counseling continued I encouraged Kevin to concentrate on the growth-producing aspects of our relationship, i.e., acceptance, my feelings of esteem for him, and his growing sense of himself as a complete male. This effort is compatible with the goals of counseling as specified by Moberly.

From the present evidence it would seem clear that the homosexual condition does not involve abnormal needs, but normal needs that have, abnormally, been left unmet in the ordinary process of growth. The needs as such are normal; their lack of fulfillment, and the barrier to their fulfillment is abnormal. Just as the problem of homosexuality is twofold, there must likewise be a twofold therapeutic goal. This twofold answer must be the undoing of the defensive detachment, and making up for unmet needs. Sexual activity may be an inappropriate solution. It is not, however, enough to discourage a mistaken solution without pointing to the proper solution, which is the meeting of same-sex needs without sexual activity. Hitherto, the Christian churches have tended to concentrate on preventing an improper response to the problem, and have failed to do much about getting started on the real answer.[4]

The counseling relationship is so important with homosexual counselees because it offers them the opportunity to work through the detachment from the same-sex parent and to develop a new identification that is not based on erotic contact. This is why careful handling of expressions of love or affection are so important. The counseling relationship may serve as a type of reparenting process by which the counselee learns that the proper relationship with the same-sex parent, and therefore other persons of the same sex, is not rejection of eroticization but love which is freely expressed without sexual activity.

DEALING WITH TRANSFERENCE AND COUNTERTRANSFERENCE

Most people who have read about Freud are aware of the terms *transference* and *countertransference*. These terms refer to feelings for other persons being transferred to the counselor (transference) or feelings from the counselor's part being transferred to the counselee (countertransference). Gary Collins has given some helpful examples.

Counselors sometimes emphasize a reaction called *transference*. This is the tendency for a counselee to have feelings toward the counselor that originally were directed toward someone else. Consider, for example, a situation in which a young counselee meets with an older male counselor. If the counselee hates his or her father, this hatred may be "transferred" to the counselor. If the counselor, in turn, begins treating the counselee like his grown son or daughter, we have a reaction termed *countertransference*.[5]

Transference

Issues of transference may be particularly significant in counseling with homosexuality because there are both positive and negative matters with which to contend.

Sandy hated her controlling mother whom she felt she could never please. Thus the first time the counselor appeared to show displeasure, Sandy became angry and hostile. "Surely you aren't going to treat me that way too, are you?" The counselor, who was somewhat surprised by the outburst, stayed calm and said, "Help me to understand what happened." After Sandy had had a chance to explain and to express her feelings even more, the counselor dealt with the transference.

"Sandy," she said, "I think you just took a great step forward. You have been angry for years about being criticized and not accepted. Today you were able to speak up for yourself. I'm glad you were able to tell me how you feel. I could even hear a little more of it. What are some other things that I or others do to you that really make you angry?"

The negative transference had opened the door to a whole new world of self-exploration for Sandy. As she talked the counselor was able to help Sandy go back to issues with her mom and express her feelings about the situation. This step was very important and it would never have happened if the counselor had taken the criticism and emotional outburst personally instead of recognizing it for what it was—negative transference.

Positive transference may also occur, especially when counselees have not been able to express their positive feelings in the past. Adam told his counselor how much he really cared for him. The counselor was careful not to push the feelings aside too quickly because he did not want to discredit them. He did, however, look for opportunities to help Adam identify other individuals who Adam loved.

Adam said, "I guess I feel like you are the dad I never really had." Adam's father had died when he was quite young and Adam has not bonded in any way with his stepfather. Adam's attachment to the counselor represented a major breakthrough toward forming new, positive relationships.

As with other important aspects of counseling, transference and countertransference must be carefully evaluated. Hurding writes,

> One of the most crucial psychological aspects of caring for our clients is that of transference and counter-transference. Once more, Kelsey is cautious. He does not believe that transference is an essential part of therapy and limits the number of counselling sessions initially in order to evaluate whether a potential transference will be constructive or destructive. He realises that clergy, doctors and therapists are sitting targets for psychological projection where, for instance, a woman parishioner or patient may invest such "authority" figures with all the strong feelings that are displaced from the repressed animus. The counsellor must treat warily, avoiding deceit or sarcasm towards the enamoured client. Even so, rightly managed, Kelsey regards transference as "one of the most creative forces in the world"—a force which, "like dynamite . . . needs to be handled with care."[6]

Countertransference

Sometimes counselors are slow to realize that they have feelings from the past that may be transferred to their counselees. I have discovered that I feel deep love for some counselees who remind me of my dad. I am also attracted to female counselees who exhibit the delightful playfulness I find in my wife. I feel empathy and compassion for counselees, and these feelings affect the way I relate to them. I am not afraid of these feelings as long as I keep them in perspective and make good choices about how they are expressed toward the counselee. I find the consultation and perspective of my colleagues very helpful at this point.

A general rule to keep in mind is that *counseling is for the counselee and not the counselor.* I might have an underlying desire to express some of the emotions I am feeling, but the key question is, what effect will it have upon the counselee and upon the counseling relationship? If the feelings you feel toward your counselee are of tenderness they may be appropriately expressed. If they are sexual in nature the expression may be counterproductive. I follow the general rule that the person with whom you discuss your intimate feelings is the one with whom you become more intimate. Thus, if sexually attracted to a counselee, I talk to a friend or my wife about it, not the counselee. Counselees have enough to deal with without having to sort out my affection needs.

Counselors who are heterosexual sometimes become confused when working with homosexual counselees because the counselor may experience feelings that he or she was not aware existed. These feelings do not mean that the counselor is a "latent homosexual." They may mean that the counselor has some unresolved issues with his or her parents. Such issues should be worked out with another counselor or friend, not the counselee.

When the countertransference issues are negative in nature, extreme care should be taken not to take out your hostility on the counselees. It is okay not to like your counselees, but it is not okay to express feelings toward them which they do not deserve. When I feel anger or uneasiness toward counselees I try to talk to myself about it. (I don't believe you can be sane unless you learn to talk to yourself.) I ask, did the counselee do anything to deserve the feelings I have or is it my problem? If I can't identify a specific offense I remind myself to go slow and not to build a case against the counselee. Often I have found that as I hold back my feelings and give myself time to understand them I find the negative feelings toward the counselee going away. Some of the counselees I started out disliking have turned out to be the ones I have become the most fond of. Be patient with yourself and patient with your counselees.

If your negative countertransference feelings do not

dissipate, you need to consider very strongly making a referral. This can be done very unobtrusively if you are factual and compassionately honest.

"Tad," the counselor said softly, "I don't feel I am doing a very good job counseling with you and I want us to talk about getting you in contact with someone who might be able to do better for you. I have some feelings from my past that I really haven't been able to set aside." After the discussion that followed, both the counselor and Tad felt good about a referral. There was no failure involved on either part. The failure would have been to fail to recognize and deal with the feelings involved.

IMPLICATIONS FOR COUNSELOR SELECTION

Our discussion of the close emotional interaction between the counselor and counselee raises an important question regarding counselor selection. Is the best counselor for the person struggling with homosexuality one of the same sex or the opposite sex?

As a general rule, I would encourage homosexuals to work with counselors of the same sex. I believe this provides the greatest opportunity for ambivalence toward the same-sex parent to be worked out. The intense relationship between the counselee and the same-sex counselor has the potential for new bonding and positive identification with the same sex. Moberly writes,

A homosexual may be helped in various ways by a counsellor of the opposite sex, but that person cannot directly help to fulfil same-sex deficits. The full potential of counselling will only be realised when the counsellor is of the same sex as the homosexual. Gender-specificity is not something arbitrary but quite simply the correlation of the solution with the exact nature of the problem. All it means is that a woman cannot be a father, and a man cannot be a mother. Thus, where the problem is specifically a deficit in fathering, a man is required to help; where the problem is specifically a deficit in mothering, it is only a woman who can make this good.[7]

169

Whenever you as a counselor must work with a homosexual counselee of the opposite sex it is essential that you get him or her involved in same-sex friendship patterns in which they may be working on the key issues mentioned above. I am working with a homosexual struggler of the opposite sex, but I am doing so with the realization that she has two close friends and confidantes of the same sex and she is also opening up issues with her sister. In this case I am of more help as a case manager than as a therapist. I do not pull back from the task, but I recognize some of its limitations.

I believe that there is a place for work with an opposite-sex counselee, particularly after an identification with the same sex has occurred and healing of the need for experiencing love and acceptance from the same sex has taken place. Many lesbian counselees have had very unfavorable experiences with men and could benefit from talking about those issues with a caring, nonbrutal man. This may be a very needed adjustment to therapy with a same-sex counselor. There may be a place for saying to your same-sex homosexual counselees, "I have been able to help you a lot to regain your sense of being a man (or woman), but now I think it is time to work on issues with the opposite sex as well. I will continue to see you but I want you to see counselor X also."

This chapter may be difficult for some readers because it deals with tough issues: issues of emotion, and of emotional confrontation. A final word of caution is in order. Do not be afraid to connect with other human beings, regardless of their problems or sexual orientation. You may not be able to solve their problems but if you follow some of the guidelines presented here you can surely be an influence in the right direction. If you need to make a referral at some point you have not failed. You have only practiced the importance of self-awareness and appropriate choices which have been advocated.

CHAPTER ELEVEN

CONFRONTING HOMOPHOBIA

THE WORD HOMOPHOBIA DOES NOT APPEAR in most dictionaries and it is even omitted from many standard lists of fears. In everyday activity, however, the term is heard quite frequently. Homosexuality is here to stay and has brought with it a new social phenomenon, homophobia, the fear of homosexuality.

Homophobia may take many forms: fear of being thought homosexual by others, fear of possible homosexual response in oneself, fear of "catching" homosexuality (as though it were a contagious disease), fear that children will see homosexuality as a viable alternative to heterosexual marriage and will choose a homosexual lifestyle, and so on.[1]

171

Homophobia affects all of us in one way or another. Those who are homosexuals or are struggling with sexual confusion fear what they might become or fear the consequences of being found out. They become fearful of being labeled and may even sabotage good relationships with same-sex friends for fear that they will be seen as strange. People are driven by their own fears, and they are also driven to deeper fear when they feel they are not understood.

Homosexuals are ridiculed by jokes or by derogatory terms like "fairy," "faggot," or "queer." Parents are fearful that any "feminine" interest shown by a boy may lead to a homosexual life so they are quick to provide footballs, toy guns, and model airplanes even if their son is not very interested in those items.[2]

Society in general fears homosexuals and often strikes out against them. We often fear most that which we do not understand.

EFFECTS OF HOMOPHOBIA

Homophobia, like other fears, creates division. It leads to a society of "good people" and "bad people" based upon a single criteria, sexual preference. Other qualities of life are ignored. Virtue and courage are rejected if they are found in the presence of the homophile condition. Such divisions affect society at large and they also affect the church. I have found mixed response to my interest in homosexuality. Some say "how can you do it?" (an obvious homophobic response). Others say "I just think it is wonderful that you are helping those poor people." The homophobia in this response is more subtle, but it is there, nevertheless. Sometimes I hear, "aren't you afraid of AIDS?" One lady asked, "are they dangerous?"

Fortunately many people in our society and within the church are not fearful. They seek to bring unity and a positive response to difference.

Where positive response to homosexuality does not exist there is alienation. People feel branded and are even fearful of

172

being hazed by their brothers and sisters in Christ. Troy Perry tells of a conversation with a friend, Carlos, who said:

"Troy, be a realist, people really don't care. Nobody likes a homosexual."
"Well, Carlos, even if people don't, I'm still convinced that God does."
Well, Carlos just laughed bitterly, and said, "Oh, come on, Troy, God doesn't care about me. I even went to my minister, and I told him I was a homosexual. Do you know what he told me? He said that I couldn't be a homosexual and a Christian too. No, Troy! God doesn't care about me!" With that he turned and left.[3]

This type of alienation is extremely harmful to both the Christian community and our outreach to society. The inconsistencies are clear. We believe that lying is a sin, and yet we reach out to the liars. We believe that adultery is a sin and find compassion for the adulterer. We believe that the practice of homosexuality is a sin and close our doors to both the practicing homosexual and the person who is trying hard to obey God. Marilyn said, "I never was accepted by the people at my church once they knew I was struggling. They weren't there to share my victories and they refused to relate to me when I needed them the most."

Alienation prevents ministry. We can't help the hurting or bring life to those who need God when they feel only our rejection. There is a better way. A Christian university student came to talk to me. He lived in a dormitory with several young men who were gay and wanted to know how to relate to them. We talked about friendship and caring. We talked about earning the right to be heard and the possibility of his being labeled. He didn't back off and he was a source of life to his friends.

"I don't see this as any different from being friends with guys who drink or people who party all the time," he said. "I have to stand up for what I believe and still be a true friend to them." I agreed with my courageous friend and tried to help him as he walked with his friends and tried to show God's love to them.

Christian ministry is the proclamation of the good news, the gospel. Jesus walked among sinners so that he could get the news out. Christian ministry also involves proclamation of the bad news. The bad news is that people are sinful and under God's condemnation. Thus they need the good news. Homophobia usually results in proclamation of only the bad news which always brings further alienation unless it is coupled with the good news.

Another negative effect of homophobia is avoidance of central issues. The alienated tend to blame those who alienate them and sometimes avoid dealing with their own choices of life. Jim was railing at a person who had spoken against gay rights. I listened and empathized until he seemed more relaxed. At that point I said, "Jim, are you avoiding?" He asked what I meant.

"I mean are you looking for things to detract you from addressing some of the issues you have to face in your life?" He thought for only a moment and then nodded affirmatively. I suggested to him that his anger over prejudice and homophobia had become an emotional scapegoat that cushioned him from having to deal with the issues.

Jim finally admitted that as long as he could find someone to blame he didn't have to address the issue of whether or not he, as a believer, should frequent gay bars. We agreed that prejudice needed to be attacked but not as a substitute for his taking charge of his own life and deciding how God wanted him to live.

HOMOPHOBIA AS FEAR OF SELF

It is terrible to feel different, to feel like you don't belong. These feelings are often paramount among people who experience crises in gender identity.

Jerome said, "I knew I was different but I didn't have the slightest idea as to what that all meant. I hated myself because I didn't know what was going on in me." I have rarely worked with a person who wanted to be a homosexual. Why would one want to be treated the way homosexuals are treated? Most homosexuals with whom I have worked have discovered that, for whatever reason, they are attracted to the same sex and that it does not go away. It is a part of their self and there are mammoth decisions to be made regarding this aspect.

Mollie said, "If this is who I am, I'm not sure I want to be. I don't know whether or not I can change and I don't know whether or not I can accept myself if I can't. I'm trapped and I don't know what to do."

It is not surprising that this type of confusion would leave a person highly stressed and sometimes unable to function. This leads to even greater fear because such persons are not sure they can cope; they even fear mental illness. They feel they are in a downward spiral for which they can see no solution.

Some people, observing this trauma, have jumped to the faulty conclusion that mental weakness, neurosis, or psychological inferiority are characteristics of homosexuals. Homosexuals are thus branded as inferior. This leads to greater homophobia both on the part of the individual and of society. I believe we have a "which came first—the chicken or the egg?" kind of problem here. Are homosexuals unable to cope because they are homosexuals or are they homosexual because they are unable to cope? The illness model promoted the idea that involvement in a homosexual lifestyle was the result of a neurotic personality. This led to great fear on the part of the homosexual and society. I believe the better view is to see the homosexual as having to cope with many stresses which society at large cannot even understand. I have worked with many who would have broken under the stress had it not been for the strength of their characters. They are brave people who labor under a heavy emotional burden.

Having said this we must also deal honestly with the fact that the breakdowns in family relationships which are seen as contributing factors to the homosexual condition have left the individuals with very stressful situations and undeveloped skills in dealing with them. Withdrawal is often used as a coping mechanism for stress. When a person struggling with the homosexual condition withdraws, his or her opportunity to learn social skills may also disappear.

> . . . homosexual persons are living in a hostile society and would have every reason to have psychological problems.

Those homosexual men and women who seek out help toward a "cure" or a change of orientation often point out that they can no longer stand being stigmatized, discriminated against, joked and sneered about, and threatened by disclosure and even blackmail. They can no longer bear having to live two lives. The strain becomes too great, the self-hatred too strong, the anxieties too engulfing.[4]

The Fear of Not Being Adequate

Homosexuals must cope with several specific fears if they are to gain a sense of wholeness. First, there is the fear of not being adequate. Pete said, "When I sit in management meetings I wonder if anyone there knows about my struggle. I think to myself *why should I speak? They won't take me seriously anyway.*" One solution and one way for Pete to deal with his personal homophobia is to focus on the fact that his sexual preference is a very, very small part of his total being. He is in the management meetings because he has been recognized as a competent manager. He is a church leader because God has gifted him with leadership abilities. He told me of a breakthrough. "I was sitting in a regional meeting quivering in my shoes when my turn came. I have as many good ideas as anyone in this meeting, I thought. I need to be heard." He spoke and found that he was taken seriously. Through this he gained more confidence. He grew to the place of having nothing to demonstrate except his skills. The sexual issue was a private matter.

Pete also spoke of his problems with church during the time he was working through his problems with homosexuality. "I felt every sermon and every Bible study had to be related to my need to decide about homosexuality. I stopped being a total spiritual person and was just a homosexual. You will never know how relieved I was the first time I heard a sermon and said to myself, 'that's for me, not because I'm a homosexual struggler but because I'm a Christian struggler.' I had put my Christian growth on hold until after I saw how the battle was going to come out. That was a big mistake."

Once Pete began to accept himself as adequate he was able to perceive his homosexual struggle as a part of him, but not *the* defining part.

The Fear of Not Being Accepted

Recognizing homophobia and the fear of not being accepted can often be a clue for the counselor of an ongoing homosexual struggle in the counselee. Sharon was continually evaluating whether or not she was accepted in group situations. If she perceived herself as not being accepted she wondered if it was because people knew of her homosexual condition. If she felt accepted she feared that she would lose this if others knew she was a homosexual. Hers was a no-win situation. She did not solve this problem until she came to the place of finding acceptance through her own self-evaluation. Galatians 6:4 and 5 were important to her in this process.

Each one should test his own actions. Then he can take pride in himself, without comparing himself to somebody else, for each one should carry his own load.

Fear of not being accepted is also accentuated by the fact that many homosexuals have been subjected to humiliation by heterosexuals and homosexuals alike. People at his school called him a "Fag." A group of homosexual men with whom he had come in contact shaved him from head to toe. Who is to say which humiliation was worse?

I do not believe that "God creates homosexuality"; but I do believe the person with the homosexual struggle is a creation of God and is, therefore, due acceptance and respect. As Christian counselors we must lead the fight to help homosexuals accept themselves and experience acceptance by others. We are called to walk the fine line which leads to acceptance of the person even when we may not condone the sexual practices. When we are able to do this we will lead people to wholeness. When people feel whole they can make better decisions.

Leanne Payne writes of steps toward self-acceptance:

There are, as the psychologists point out, progressions from infancy to maturity which involve steps of "psychosocial development." When we miss one of these normal progressions, we are in trouble.

177

One of the progressions vital to this matter of self-acceptance is the step *from* the narcissistic period of puberty, that "autoerotic," self-centered phase when one's attention is more or less painfully centered on one's own body and self, *to* that developmental level whereby one has accepted himself and has turned his eyes and heart outward toward all else in the created world. To whatever degree one fails in regard to this step, he will find himself stuck in some form or manifestation of the wrong kind of self-love. Failing to love himself aright, he will love himself amiss.[5]

The Fear of Not Reaching Life Goals

A third fear homosexuals have, which contributes to their own homophobia, is the fear of not reaching certain life goals. Steve said, "I really want a wife and children, but I can't marry for that alone. The sexual part has to be resolved first." Many homosexuals have made the mistake of marriage, assuming they can reach these goals or to prove that they are "normal." These decisions usually lead to disaster because they leave the real problem unaddressed. Successful marriage is possible after resolution of the struggle, not as a step in resolution.

There are other goals which homosexuals may be fearful of not reaching: career goals, such as the ministry, or financial security, social acceptance—even constitutionally based freedoms.

The homosexual also fears the unknown; and this strengthens his or her homophobia. "What will become of me?" a young woman asked pleadingly. "Can anyone tell me where this thing will end?" I responded by helping her see that although there were some things she could not control, there were also many things she could. "You will become whom you choose to become. If you choose to withdraw you will become a recluse. If you choose to go to college you will become a college grad. If you choose to be a Christian you will become a child of God. If you choose to engage in the lesbian lifestyle you will be a lesbian. If you choose to explore growth and change you will grow and change. The choices are yours. You cannot control everything, but you can control more than you realize."

As a counselor you are a guide for your homosexual counselees. You are leading them into the unknown. You have the advantage of your experience with others and can direct them to choices that will keep open their possibilities for life. Don't be afraid to encourage homosexual counselees to keep their options open. Homosexuality is a problem, not a curse.

Every counselor encounters prejudice. As you counsel homosexuals you will hurt with them while they talk of the effects which fear of homosexuality has had upon their lives. The experience of having someone turn completely away when he or she learns that the counselee is struggling with sexual identity is a very devastating thing. Shelly said, "I felt like my heart was being cut out. Cindy and I had been friends for years and now she doesn't ever call me. It's like once she found out that I was struggling she wrote me off. Don't all those good years mean anything to her?"

I find I need to address five areas as I help counselees who are facing the effects of homophobia.

The first is helping them keep their perspective on their self-worth. This was addressed in the previous section. I disagree with many things that the Reverend Troy Perry has written, but I believe the title of one of his books is a useful focus for persons facing homophobia. That title is *The Lord Is My Shepherd and He Knows I'm Gay.* Being gay is a difficult dilemma for thousands of Christian people. However, the homosexual condition does not change the fact that God loves them and shepherds them. They have value. They belong to him.

Next, I have to teach counselees to let prejudiced people have their problem. The homosexual does not create the prejudice, fear does. Thus, persons with the fear are the ones with the problem. Letting them have their problem doesn't mean that your counselee will no longer hurt, but it does mean that he or she does not have to add guilt to the list of hurts. Bill was finally able to say, "I can't solve this for him. I have to decide what to do with me and he has decisions to make for himself."

Third, counselees need to be taught how to confront prejudice. Most of my homosexual counselees are either shy or angry or both. They lack the skills in the middle. They need to learn how to assert themselves without attacking the other person. I asked Shelly if she thought she could call Cindy and tell her that she missed seeing her and wondered if they could get together for a time to talk about what had happened. I coached her in assertiveness so that by the time they met she was able to tell Cindy more of what she was feeling. This was probably one of the few times Shelly had ever told someone else what she was feeling. I taught her to use "I" statements, such as "I feel hurt" or "I miss you," as opposed to attacks, such as "you have run out on me." I taught her to clarify the communication so Cindy would know how much of the rumored talk to believe. This led to a restoration of the relationship. Cindy was still a little uncertain, but she was willing to stay in the relationship. Confronting prejudice will not always take it away, but it can help minimize the damage.

Fourth, counselees need help to avoid the temptation to overcompensate, to try to make up for what they see as deficient in themselves. Dick related, "For months after my homosexual struggle was known at church I felt like I had to make it up to all my friends. I had not hurt them, but somehow I felt like I had to do something to be good enough to be accepted again. I was frantic, like a man trying to climb a hill that is too steep." Dick's friend had helped him get back to sanity. He said, "Dick, why are you doing all this? I don't need it in order to be your friend. You don't have to make me like you now that I know. I haven't stopped liking you from before."

Lastly, counselees need help to avoid the temptation to run. When people don't treat you kindly there is always the thought, *I can't stand this. I have to get away.* Sometimes the withdrawal is deliberate; at other times it is more subtle or even subconscious. Your counselees may even withdraw from you.

Keith had not been to see me for some time. After canceling an appointment for a good reason he did not keep his promise to set another. Finally, I called him to see what was going on. After some avoidance he said, "I guess I'm afraid of talking to anyone. I haven't been to church for a month. I'm afraid I can't deal with it." I challenged him not to isolate himself and asked him to set another appointment. Slowly but surely he began to reinvolve himself with life in general; this was difficult for him and it took a lot of encouragement from me. Sometimes the counselor may have to ask a counselee to call a friend who will go with him or her to the session. In the most difficult situations you may have to call the friend for your counselee. It is important that you as a counselor do not become so professional that you cease to be caring and supportive. You cannot carry counselees. There must be movement on their part. You can, however, give them a lift or a push to get them going.

TAKING A STAND

Counselors are social activists whether they like it or not. You have to stand up for what you believe and you have to stand up for your clients.

Occasionally I hear statements, even from church leaders, which tend to ignite homophobia. Reference to homosexuals as "idiots" is a good example. I cannot let such references go unchallenged. I have to say, "Excuse me. Homosexuals are not idiots. They are bright, caring people who are faced with some very hard choices. We may not understand them and we may not agree with them personally or politically, but let's not brand them."

I also find it necessary to publicly challenge untrue statements, such as "boys who play with dolls will become homosexuals," or "homosexuals are rapists and child molestors." These statements are not true anymore than their opposites are true: "boys who play with dolls will become heterosexuals" or, "heterosexuals are rapists and child molesters." These statements stem from homophobia and they generate even more homophobia. We have to stand up against them.

Take a stand by taking a positive approach. Spread information that heals, not poisons. Urge your pastor to share a message of hope and redemption, not condemnation. Get him or her to challenge the congregation to get involved in close relationships with others, including homosexuals. Friendship and nonerotic love are the homosexual's greatest needs. We dare not fall down on our responsibility; especially, we dare not fail because of our own homophobia.

Another area of homophobia that we Christians must face is our fear and suspicion about close same-sex friendships. How can we expect the world to "know that we are Christ's disciples by our love for one another" if we're *afraid* to love each other because somebody might think we're homosexual? Persons who are basically heterosexual need to realize that affectionate feelings towards friends of the same sex do not necessarily entail *erotic* feelings. There is no reason, because of simply feeling affection, to fear that one is somehow "becoming" homosexual. It is certainly possible to feel and speak of love for someone else without the slightest desire to express that love through genital sexual relations.[6]

CHAPTER TWELVE

AIDS, THE DREADED KILLER

AIDS, THE DREADED KILLER, is receiving more attention than cancer. It is a threat to our society and is being addressed from many directions. How is it to be addressed here? My choice has been to approach AIDS from the direction I know best, discussing the psychological struggles of the individual client. How do you counsel as you face the people and the families who have been affected?

Because of the vast amount of materials that are available to explain the disease and its dangers I have chosen to guide the reader to some of those materials rather than try to include them here. Also, I have not addressed the ethical and sociological implications. These issues demand attention from those who specialize in such important concerns. Parenthetically, I have noticed that books on homosexuality which deal with ethical considerations all seem to have been written prior to AIDS. Who will speak to these issues?

Jim sat quietly as I asked him about his sexual orientation and the choices he was making. He seemed comfortable with his gay lifestyle and he didn't hesitate to let me know that he wasn't inhibited by any of this "religious stuff." He seemed almost defiant as he unabashedly stated what he believed to be the advantages of his "coming out" and living the kind of life that is authentic for him.

Inevitably we got to the topic of AIDS. As I raised the question, I could see the tension mount in his body; tears began to form in his eyes. "That's a very tender subject for me," he said. "I lost a close friend this week." Nodding in sympathy I allowed him to speak. He wanted to talk about his friend and the hurt that he felt. He spoke of the agony of watching a person die and the helplessness he felt each day as he went to visit him.

"It's too close to ignore," he said. "I just can't say it will never bother me or my friends. It is here and it has changed us."

I asked him to elaborate on the changes he saw. "It really hasn't changed our commitment to a lifestyle," he remarked, "but it has changed our behavior in the bedroom." He talked of the dangers of cruising and sex with strangers. He related how important were conversations concerning "safe sex," and talked of a trend toward monogamous relationships. He wistfully spoke of a cure someday.

"In the meantime," he said, "we have to protect ourselves. In that regard we aren't really different from the heterosexuals out there. There is an enemy that has changed the sexual revolution."

Researchers have identified two sets of issues that must be addressed with AIDS counselees: short-term reactions and long-term issues. The short-term reactions include shock, anger, anxiety, depression, and sexual dysfunction. The long-term issues are existential and spiritual issues, relationship concerns, and issues related to the past.[1]

Those who counsel with homosexuals will deal with four groups of people with regards to AIDS: (1) the practicing homosexual who is fearful of catching the disease; (2) the person who has contracted the disease and is facing death; (3) the family of the homosexual who must deal with their fears that their son, daughter, or spouse may acquire the disease, and (4) the family of the person dying of AIDS. The task is not an easy one but as counselors we dare not shirk our responsibilities.

WORKING WITH THE FEAR OF CONTRACTING AIDS

There are times when fears are justified, and a practicing homosexual's fear of contracting AIDS certainly falls into that category. People who are regularly having sex with strangers or persons whom they don't really know very well are at great risk. You may not convince your counselees that abstinence is possible for them, but they must be helped to think through behavior plans so that they are not ruled only by their impulse to have sex.

It is the counselor's responsibility to get helpful information into the hands of the counselee and then to make sure that the material has been understood correctly. An adolescent counselee told me that he had been practicing safe sex. My first thought was that that sounded okay: He is going to be sexually active; at least he is smart enough to protect himself. My next thought was more productive. I realized I had to know exactly what he was saying to me.

"What does safe sex mean to you?" I asked.

"I don't have intercourse," he said. "I just have oral sex and I don't let the sperms get in my mouth."

I pursued. "Do you mean you and your partner always wear a condom?"

"Well, not always," he replied.

"How about wet kissing?" I asked. "Is that safe?"

"I think so!" he said.

"'Think so' is not adequate," I asserted. "Let's check on what the authorities are saying."

A chart from the pamphlet "Safe Sex,"[2] distributed by the American College Health Association, was most helpful in showing the counselee that two of his "safe sex" practices actually fell into the risky category. Confrontation, using such authoritative material, is much more powerful than the counselor's trying to dispute the counselee's beliefs verbally. In effect, letting him see the chart was forcing him to confront his own misperceptions and discover for himself that he was wrong.

Some counselors may object to the idea of teaching about "safe sex," believing that, biblically, they should be teaching that the practice of homosexuality is wrong and that sex outside of marriage is wrong. I am sympathetic with this position, and I believe that the only truly safe sex is with a single partner, one's spouse. We must recognize, however, that many of our counselees may be out of control sexually or unwilling to accept an abstinence position. Many recognized Christian leaders, like the Surgeon-General of the United States, Everett Koop, have stressed the need to use condoms even though they believe the best choice is abstinence. I believe that we as counselors have an obligation to help counselees evaluate their sexual practices and make better choices even though they may not be willing to make what we would consider the wisest choice of all—not practicing their homosexuality.

When there has been sexual contact, counselees may be unaware of the need for testing for the AIDS virus; or they may be unaware of how to get the needed tests. You as a counselor need to know where tests can be acquired and be willing even to take your counselees if they are too fearful.

Do not allow people to suffer under the fear of the unknown. The sooner they know one way or the other the sooner they will be able to make productive decisions regarding the next steps in their lives.

WORKING WITH THOSE FACING DEATH

Be Prepared to Deal with Grief

Recently I received a call from a representative of an employee assistance program of a large company in our area. The representative said, "I have a possible referral for you, but first I need to ask you some questions." Her questions were: "Are you willing to work with someone who has AIDS?" and, "Do you understand Christian beliefs enough to help persons work through their anger, doubts, and grief?"

The man she referred was a believer who had acquired AIDS through a blood transfusion. He was afraid, bitter, and angry with God. He had tried to grieve alone but wasn't doing very well. He was full of questions for which he had not been able to find answers, and was struggling with feelings of shame even though he knew he had done nothing wrong. "I must be a terrible person," he told me later, "or God would not have let this happen."

Grief is a response to a loss. In the case of AIDS victims, it is a response to impending loss of life. It is amazing how even people who have been suicidal become frantic when their lives are threatened. Life is a gift from God and it is very upsetting when that gift may be taken away.

Mary said, "The worst part was the realization that many of my dreams may never come true." Others have had to face issues of eternity and God which they had been able to avoid until the reality of death hit them. These issues must be addressed directly by the counselor. One person said, "Counselors are always telling us how to live, but now it looks like they are going to have to help us learn how to die."

Counselors who deal with death and disease need to be familiar with grief counseling literature and techniques. We must learn to listen to our counselees' concerns and to help them talk about their feelings. We must help them focus on their losses.

One loss may loom very large for the Christian homosexual—feelings of being abandoned by God. "Where is God in all this?" is a common question. There are issues that need to be explored. Why did God let this happen? This is usually an issue when the AIDS victim feels that contracting the disease was not his or her fault. Parents and friends also feel this way as they try to understand how it could have happened to their loved one. I find it helpful to explain to counselees that the rain falls on the just and the unjust (Matt. 5:45), and so does evil. I do not believe that God singles people out to be homosexual and I do not believe he selects people to plague with AIDS. I also remind people that God does not promise to deliver us from trouble, but does promise not to forsake us in our trouble.

Yea, though I walk through the valley of the shadow of death, I fear no evil; for thou art with me; thy rod and thy staff they comfort me. (Ps. 23:4, KJV)

These explanations are not always adequate to answer all the questions counselees have. But they do give them some new ideas to consider which may lead them out of pity or self-condemnation and back toward a God who cares. I encourage people to share all their feelings with God, even their anger, and then to listen as he ministers to them. "Draw nigh to God and he will draw nigh to you" (James 4:8a KJV) is helpful for some to consider.

The question of punishment and forgiveness must also be addressed. As I stated above, some who contract AIDS are victims, just as some who are crippled in automobile accidents are blameless.

God does punish the unrepentant, but even those who have repented may discover that they have AIDS. Sin has natural consequences such as AIDS, but the presence of AIDS does not mean that God has singled that person out for punishment. Neither does it mean that the AIDS victim's sins have not been forgiven. Repentance and forgiveness mean that the person is free from the judgment of God. Christ died for their sins and those sins are washed away. This does not mean, however, that forgiven sinners won't die of AIDS, or cancer, or of some accident.

Those who are struggling with guilt must be led to receive forgiveness from God so they can live in such a way as to prepare them for life eternal with God. First John 4:18 emphasizes that perfect love drives out fear.

There is no fear in love. But perfect love drives out fear, because fear has to do with punishment. The man who fears is not made perfect in love.

The "perfect love" is God's forgiving love. The fear is the fear of death. The wise counselor will help people find that forgiveness and thus be able either to live or die in peace knowing that God's love for them is strong and that he has not abandoned them.

There is a third type of grieving which AIDS victims experience. This is a grief over loss of normal relationships. People withdraw from AIDS victims just as though they were lepers. Vern said, "My friends don't come around any more. In fact, they don't even call on the telephone. I guess they think I could infect them by long distance." He tried to be funny but could not mask the deep hurt he was feeling. I tried to respond to the hurt. "People just don't understand how badly you need them right now, do they Vern?" I said. He nodded and the tears began to flow. The need for maintenance of normal contact with the AIDS patient cannot be overlooked.

Be Prepared to Offer Practical Help

When people are ill they need their friends more than ever. Unfortunately, the friends and even family may be too wrapped up in their own fears and/or grief to respond. There are three things that you as a counselor can do to help.

1. You may need to intervene directly by contacting key people who have withdrawn from your counselee. I believe counselors must be advocates at times, because grieving people aren't always able to care for themselves.

Doug was shy and had a very low self-image, long before he contracted AIDS. He could not tell his brother how much he needed him. He could not tell his friends how much a visit or a telephone call would help. His counselor needed to step in and do it for him.

2. You will need to teach your counselees how to state their own needs clearly so that others will know how to relate to them. Grieving people often make the mistake of thinking that others should know. This results in an unwillingness to tell others what they need because then the response may not seem genuine. This is a mistake that you must teach your counselees not to make. I sometimes use role-playing as a tool to help teach people assertiveness.

"Nat," I said, "I want you to tell me exactly what you wish your friends would do." He struggled for a while because, like most people who are grieving, he wasn't able to verbalize his needs. After some time, however, he was able to put his feelings into words. The next step was to be able to tell me in the same way he would tell his friends.

"No," I said, "let me be your friend Jack and you tell me like you need to tell him." He nodded reluctantly. I responded by handing him a make-believe telephone with instructions to give Jack a call. I answered his call almost before he could finish dialing.

"Hello, this is Jack."

"Hi Jack, this is Nat. I've been thinking about you so I decided to give you a call."

Jack: "Thanks. How are you doing?"

Nat: "Okay I guess."

Jack: "That's good."

Nat: "Actually I've been feeling kind of lonely and I need to tell you about it."

Jack: "Okay."

Nat: "I'm not mad at you and my other friends, but it does seem like you have backed off from being my friend. I don't think I've had a telephone call for quite some time."

Jack: "You're probably right. I don't think it is intentional, but all of us feel pretty awkward. I suppose we don't know what to say or are afraid of saying the wrong thing."

Nat: "I understand that. I don't know what to say some times either. One thing you could say is 'How about going to the movie with me Saturday? We haven't done anything together for a long time.'"

Jack: "I see." (I pause, forcing Nat to continue).

Nat: "Even though I'm dealing with the possibility of death, I've decided to try to live as normally as possible. Some days I don't feel like doing much of anything but I am always ready to talk."

Jack: "I probably avoid talking to you sometimes because I feel almost guilty that I'm healthy and having a good time. I'm afraid if I share that with you it might just make you feel worse."

Nat: "It might, but it will also make me feel better. I can't handle being excluded."

Role-playing, such as the example above, gives the counselee an opportunity to learn to express needs and develop skills. It also gives the counselor opportunity to address some issues such as attitudes which may be more difficult to take head-on. For example, if I had tried to convince Nat that Jack would probably understand his loneliness and that Jack would probably be honest about some of his own feelings he might have denied or resisted my views. He was able to receive new input, however, when it was presented indirectly in the role-playing.

3. You will need to teach your counselees how to nurture themselves and to receive nurturance from God even when other people do not respond. The concept of self-nurturance is foreign to many of us because we have been raised to believe that all of our needs are to be met by others, or just ignored. Taking care of ourselves is often seen as selfish or even non-Christian. This is carried to such an extreme that many people do not even give themselves the advantage of the sabbath which is one of God's provisions for nurturing and restoring us. Rest is not a selfish option. It is a command from God. Recent research at the University of Delaware has shown the importance of spending time with nature as a means of dealing with stress. Sitting and watching a tree can be very therapeutic.

AIDS victims and their families need to learn to manage stress. The pressures of pain and uncertainty take their toll. Time to be alone and time alone with God are very important.

Those struggling with AIDS, or the effects of AIDS upon friends or family, must also learn to deal with their feelings. Keeping those feelings inside does not allow people to deal with grief. They need to talk about their feelings. Teach counselees to find someone who will listen, or teach them to listen to themselves by writing down their feelings. This is one of the best self-nurturance activities in which a person can engage.

I take time to help people understand that my telling people I have needs does not weaken the love they show when they respond to my needs. In fact, it takes more love to do what people ask of you than it does to try to guess what they need. Counselees need to know that people cannot read their minds.

Self-nurturance involves: doing things one enjoys, taking time to be refreshed, spending time with nature, dealing with one's feelings, and finding meaningful activities. People who are dying need to keep on living. When people disengage from life they die. People can be taught to take care of themselves. This will not totally take the place of support from others, but as people become more self-sufficient their confidence grows.

WORKING WITH FAMILIES WHO FEAR AIDS

When families first learn that a loved one is homosexual they are often gripped with fear. They fear both the homosexual condition which they don't understand and the possibility of a loved one contracting AIDS.

The immediate response is to want someone to straighten the family member out, or to talk some sense into him or her. When this fails, as it invariably does, the family becomes more desperate and depressed. It is at this point that family members often seek counseling. Several needs can be identified.

First, there is the need for *information.* Family members need someone with whom they can check out their information. Secondly, they need *assurance.* This is a delicate problem for counselors because we cannot promise them that everything will turn out right. We can only assure them that we will do what we can to provide a safe influence if given the chance. Sometimes homosexual counselees are committed to self-destruction and neither the counselor nor the family can change that.

Ruth Mohr discusses a family with whom she dealt. The husband, John, who was dying of AIDS, had chosen to use drugs as his way of trying to deal with his grief.

Sometimes dysfunctional systems cannot be made functional: the damage is too great, the rigidity too integral. When hope, the great lever of therapeutic change, is gone, the therapist must redefine what change is possible. At this point, John has committed himself to his own self-destruction. I have had to face the realization that there is

192

too much family history to undo in too short a space of time. And, for John, drugs have become the solution to the problem of how to face the remainder of his life. I have had to do what any clinician dealing with AIDS cases must do—define what is realistically possible to accomplish given the clients' circumstances. In this case, my hope is to help Mary and John break the pattern of dysfunction so that it is not transmitted to the next generation. My work now is organized around two goals. One is encouraging John to leave behind a more hopeful legacy for his children, imparting his dreams of a better life for them. The other is to help Mary face the practical questions of how to best provide for her children once he is gone.[3]

Thirdly, family members who fear AIDS need *a sense of direction*. They need to feel that they are taking the right steps. Here is a brief outline you might wish to share with families. I usually present it as some things they can do.

1. Continue to love and pray for your family member.
2. Spend time with him or her whenever possible.
3. Pray for the person regularly.
4. Let the person talk about his or her feelings.
5. State your position and then don't moralize.

A fourth issue usually needs to be addressed and that is the issue of *responsibility*. Families who care usually feel responsible. You need to help them to see that their loved one is making a choice and they cannot take the responsibility for that choice. Heaping guilt upon themselves will not solve the problem. Listen to family members' anguish and then tenderly direct them to forgiving themselves and letting their loved one be responsible for his or her own choices.

WORKING WITH GRIEVING AIDS FAMILIES

The counselor is often called upon to work with grieving families of AIDS victims as well as the victims themselves. Families need support and they need help in articulating their feelings about the predicament of their loved ones. As a counselor you can play an important role in both of these areas. Families need to be supported so that they can give support.

Dr. Susan Holck, medical officer in the World Health Organization, writes:

Surely one of the most difficult aspects of AIDS for families is the enormous psychological burden it places on them. In some areas of the world, AIDS carries with it such a social stigma that people with AIDS are ostracized from society. It is very difficult for families to continue to provide comfort and support in the face of such social pressure, yet, for the person with AIDS it is vital to have that continued support.

Like other sexually transmitted diseases, AIDS can bring to light non-monogamous sexual relationships, the potential implications of which will vary by culture and family, but which can be devastating. Finally, since there is no cure for AIDS, when AIDS infection is diagnosed, families have to confront the likelihood of early death and its ramifications. This is never easy, and AIDS is no exception.[4]

Counselors, especially pastoral counselors, need to be especially sensitive to family members' needs and become aggressive in establishing contacts so that needs can be expressed. When you serve the family you serve your counselee. It may become very time consuming, but it will be worth it because of the positive impact this will have on your counselees.

Treat family members the same way you treat your counselees. Help them deal with their feelings, provide emotional support, and put them in contact with others who will understand their needs and relate to their pain.

As the number of identified AIDS families grows, counselors can use group techniques as well as individual contact in order to provide healing opportunities for the family members. Some support groups for AIDS victims provide opportunity for family members to come together periodically in order to learn and to meet others who share their unique pain. I believe this can be very helpful.

Where there is much adversity there is much opportunity. In the case of AIDS, the counselor has the opportunity to minister to people in the depth of despair. As a counselor you are in a position to trust God and then step by faith into the gap. With God's help you will bring a breath of life to the dying.

There are several specific areas which you as a counselor can help families address.

1. Dealing with the social stigma. Families have to deal with such questions as whether to tell children or distant relatives. They fear attack and rejection from neighbors. In general they need help in dealing with fear and prejudice.

2. Dealing with saying good-bye. Dick and Nancy sat stunned as their counselor asked them how they wanted to say good-bye to their son. "I don't want to," Nancy cried out. "I want him to live."

"So do I," the counselor said empathetically, "but the truth is he may be gone in a few months. AIDS is a cruel death but unlike an accident you do have a chance to say good-bye and to help your son as he prepares for his death."

Dick and Nancy were encouraged to talk to each other about saying good-bye and also to talk to their son. It was difficult but important to the grieving process for all of them. They decided on a collection of positive memories which they put in a scrapbook and shared with their son. He liked it and it was displayed at his funeral. It has become a painful but valued family treasure.

3. Dealing with rebuilding lives which remain. The family does not die of AIDS; a beloved family member does. What about the rest of the family who remain behind?

I tell families that it is time for a new chapter in life. The loved one died in the last chapter. "How is the next chapter to read?" I ask. "Will it indicate function or dysfunction? Will it read depression or productivity? Will it read love or hate? Will it read bitterness or greater sensitivity to others' pain?" These questions can be very helpful to families who are trying to reform their lives after loss. As a counselor you will need to discover ways of assisting people in moving beyond their grief to new steps in life.

WHAT ABOUT YOU?

Thus far we have talked of AIDS victims and families of AIDS victims. We have stressed the importance of reaching out to these who are hurting. But what about you? Don't you have feelings too? Aren't you afraid? Are you aware of some of your own biases? Are you sure you even want to work with this problem?

Understanding Your Own Fears and Bias

Regardless of the amount of news media coverage on AIDS, we still are a long way from understanding the disease. Where there is ignorance there is usually fear. And where fear is, there will be talk, which only serves to create more fear. The fear epidemic will certainly exceed the extent of the epidemic resulting from the spread of the virus. None of us will remain untouched by fear although, hopefully, only a few of us will be affected by the virus. Notice these statistics.

> Two of every 3 new AIDS cases still involve gays, but the killer is rapidly closing in on drug users—and on heterosexuals, who by 1991 will account for 1 in 11 new cases. Official projections may be much too low. The U.S. has moved uncertainly toward recognizing the threat and dealing with it. And since AIDS is usually spread by people free of symptoms, you can't tell who's safe and who's not. In the next weeks, 220 people will die of AIDS, and 374 more—28 of them heterosexuals—will be infected with the killer virus.[5]

When you work with people in danger you feel the danger yourself. I remember vividly my feelings the first time I shook hands with a client after the session during which I learned there was a high probability that he had AIDS. I was amazed at how quickly the fear led to irrational, uncontrolled thoughts. I wondered if he had washed his hands after going to the bathroom. I thought about saliva on his fingers. I reminded myself to wash my hands immediately after he left. I wasn't just thinking of normal hygienic precautions. I was afraid for my very life. Later, I found myself hoping that he would miss his next appointment. The fear level stayed high for quite some time.

Fear is normally accompanied by bias and prejudice. *Why am I turning against this man?* I asked myself. *I like him and he is a decent human being.* This little chat with myself started the process of facing my fear. I was now able to deal with reality. I affirmed my belief that the risk was low and I reaffirmed my commitment to this counselee and others who may be suffering from AIDS. The bottom line was: *I will be as careful as good sense requires, but I will not be destroyed as a helper by fear or prejudice.* I determined to keep abreast of the latest factual information regarding the spread of the disease without withdrawing from the spiritual and psychological needs of those who face death daily. The following words from Ed Hurst helped me stay on target.

> While the AIDS epidemic is certainly a tragedy, a greater tragedy has been revealed as the epidemic grows. Many Christians are calling AIDS "God's judgment on the gays" and are self-righteously gloating that the gays "are getting what they deserve." Some gays are blaming Christians and other conservative-minded individuals for their dilemma. They see us as the source of intolerance and oppression that pushes them towards multiple partners (and hence, the greater risk of AIDS). They also see us as the major obstacle to the release of government funding for AIDS research and for prohibiting education about AIDS. They blame our "hysterical" reaction to AIDS on homophobia (fear of homosexuals).[6]

The current AIDS hysteria cannot be blamed entirely on homophobia or homosexual oppression. A certain hysteria surrounded the outbreak of polio in this country. A similar hysteria began to emerge after the second outbreak of Legionnaire's Disease. Some of the hysteria is a natural fear of death and the unknown.

Have the Best Possible Information Available

As a counselor you may be asked questions about AIDS or sexuality in general which you cannot answer. A counseling rule will help you here: *When in doubt, refer, or help the person acquire the needed information.*

If you are not qualified to give medical advice or answer

questions about human sexuality then you need to develop resources which can be made available. If you live in a large metropolitan area you will need to know where to refer people for AIDS testing and who are the best doctors who can discuss options, if a counselee has the disease. Referral sources are needed for diagnosis, treatment, and support for the person and family. Being a good source of information will help you build confidence with your counselees.

The counselor must deal with his or her own ignorance and fear and must also deal with the counselees' and their families' and friends' emotions and lack of information. Street information is never enough. The counselor needs to be armed with the results of medical research and the best thinking of persons in the field. A list of helpful materials and sources of information will be presented in the appendix.

CHAPTER THIRTEEN

MOBILIZING THE FORCES OF THE CHURCH

IN MANY CASES the problem of homosexuality is a family problem. It is a problem within the church, the family of God. This is both good news and bad news. The bad news is that we don't like to see our brothers and sisters struggle and hurt and we don't like to see the family disrupted or thrown into a state of confusion. The good news is we have a God who cares about such problems and we also have many resources within the church which can be brought to bear upon the problem. I am challenged by my pastor's statement: "If we are not a church family who can approach the real problems that people face and somehow be instruments of redemptive healing for those people, then we are not being the church God wants us to be." Atkinson states the challenge succinctly.

Frequently homosexually oriented Christians, where their dispositions are known, have received suspicion at best, and sometimes open hostility, ridicule or worse from Christian congregations. Many therefore feel forced to keep their sexual preferences secret for fear of misunderstanding or recrimination. "No wonder," says J. Kleinig, "that gay churches have begun to emerge. Misguided though their theology may be, they stand as a judgement on the fellowship of believers."[1]

Persons who struggle with issues related to homosexuality have several specific needs that the church can meet. In this chapter we will look at a number of these needs and, where possible, make suggestions for appropriate action.

LOVE, ACCEPTANCE, AND ENCOURAGEMENT

The challenge of love and acceptance was set down forcefully by Paul, who said, "Therefore, as we have opportunity, let us do good to all people, especially to those who belong to the family of believers" (Gal. 6:10).

The writer of Hebrews calls the church to a ministry of encouragement:

Let us hold unswervingly to the hope we profess, for he who promised is faithful. And let us consider how we may spur one another on toward love and good deeds. Let us not give up meeting together, as some are in the habit of doing, but let us encourage one another—and all the more as you see the Day approaching.   (Heb. 10:23–25)

Homosexuals are often without hope. These verses tell us that we are to hold on to hope and pass it on to others. We need to hold out hope to those strugglers within our family and to those who are not yet members of God's family. We need to spur one another to love and good deeds. Spurs are used for guiding the horse, not for punishment. We can direct people to God's ways without developing a punitive attitude.

I asked a friend who professes to be gay why he went to a particular church. His answer was instructive. "They don't all understand me," he said, "and they don't all approve of the way I live, but they accept me and they haven't given up on me."

The verses cited above mention two other points that have direct application to ministering to persons with same-sex preference—meet together and encourage. Jim and Margaret have friends who are struggling in their marriage. The problem is, the husband is gay. The two love each other but the wife is fearful that she will be replaced by a man, and the husband doesn't know whether or not he can continue to live with his wife when he is not sexually attracted to her. They need help. Jim and Margaret don't have all the answers, but they do care and they are determined not to leave their friends without support. They socialize together with the couple, and they go to church together when the other couple will go. And they spend a lot of time talking. Only God knows whether or not their efforts will be successful, but one thing is certain. Their encouragement can't hurt and if it is withdrawn, the couple will be without any resources. Margaret and Jim don't try to do the counseling; they don't feel comfortable in this area. However, through their efforts the couple was encouraged to seek professional help, which they are doing now. Margaret said, "What we do seems like so little, but it is at least something." I am challenged by the fact that our Lord takes delight in taking a little and turning it into a lot (see Matthew 15:29–39).

I believe that the church that takes its mission seriously will seek out those persons who may be the most needy and will try to encourage them in the things of God. In order to do this we must decide that all persons are welcome in our fellowship.

Our church has an active ministry to Cambodian refugees. It was a decision we made. At first, the situation was awkward and the people didn't know what to say or how to act. As time has gone on the church family understands the Cambodians better and we are even beginning to reach out to meet some of their needs. The same thing will have to happen in churches that want to minister to homosexuals who may be in their midst. This usually begins with a decision to be friendly.

Encouragement is a complex concept. It can be very general or very specific. It can involve commendation for what people are doing or it can involve challenging people to trust God in new ways. General encouragement is easy. It often involves little more than a smile or a pat on the back. Unfortunately, those in our midst who are struggling with same-sex preference may get neither.

When it comes to specific encouragement the task becomes more difficult. I need to decide what actions or attitudes I want to encourage. I like to encourage people to be active in worship. I encourage Bible study and prayer. I encourage people to avoid sin, if I know the sin with which they may be wrestling.

Recently I said to a friend, "I want to challenge you to stay away from downtown for a week. Each time you go there you get sexually involved and then your relationship with Christ takes a nose dive. You don't need that. You don't need any more guilt." He agreed and he was successful for five days. He avoided me for a while and when I finally saw him he reluctantly told me the story. I encouraged him by reminding him that he had made it for five days. I challenged him to go for six next time. He did and eventually that part of his life became less and less important. I involved him with me in some other activities and got him involved with other people. All of this was a part of his eventual healing.

Many people hesitate to use the word *love* to describe how they feel toward people who either sell "love" or engage in sexual activity that is condemned by the Bible. The problem is that these people who sell love are often the ones who need true love the most.

The highest form of love is *agape*, the love that has not been earned, which our Lord showed to us. This is the type of love about which the homosexual usually knows nothing. It is also the type of love that when given pierces the soul. C. S. Lewis wrote,

God is love. Again, "Herein is love, not that we loved God but that He loved us" (I *John* IV, 10). We must not begin with mysticism, with the creature's love for God, or with the wonderful foretastes of the fruition of God vouchsafed

202

to some in their earthly life. We begin at the real beginning, with love as the Divine energy. This primal love is Gift-love. In God there is no hunger that needs to be filled, only plenteousness that desires to give.[2]

Homosexuals have usually been deprived of *agape* (sacrificial love) and *phileo* (brotherly love) and have been told that *eros* is all there is. Unfortunately, they have been led into the erotic but the love has been missing.

When I told a lesbian friend that I love her she said, "I don't understand that, but I believe it and I thank you for it." A male friend who is gay said, "It's nice to have love that isn't complicated by sex."

Jesus offered the supreme challenge: "A new commandment I give you: Love one another. As I have loved you, so you must love one another. All men will know that you are my disciples if you love one another" (John 13:34, 35).

FRIENDSHIP

Providing friendship as a means of meeting the needs of people who struggle with same-sex preference is highly important. Perhaps it would be no overstatement to say the need for homosexuals to have nonsexual friendships with persons of their same sex is the greatest need they have.

Dr. Elizabeth Moberly has stated that "the fulfilment of unmet needs will require the time and active concern of a continuing relationship. It may be said that 'the conclusion of a prayer for inner healing usually involves a filling with God's love of all the empty places in our hearts.' The fulfilment of this prayer will in many instances be mediated through human channels, as prayer and relationships normally complement each other to forward the process of psychological healing."[3]

Most persons with same-sex preference feel that they don't fit in with others. They have trouble finding individuals or groups who will accept them. Some report that the opposite sex doesn't want to waste time with them and those of the same sex are afraid of being identified with them. Even persons who are not identified as homosexual report that they struggle with feelings of isolation because they fear that as soon as others find out about their struggle they will then be rejected. They bear a tremendous burden.

C. S. Lewis defines friends as "persons who see the same thing." Strugglers with homosexuality are often so engrossed in looking at issues related to their struggle that they forget about the rest of their lives. Friends encourage one another to see life in its broadest perspective and to expand their world of possibilities. Same-sex friends often do this by helping a person realize that he or she is more man or woman than he or she thinks.

Ray said, "My friendship with Phil has made me feel more normal. When I talk with him I feel legitimate. He supports the male aspects of my person which my father either denied or minimized." Carol said, "My friend Judy gives me balance. She lets me know that it is okay to be needy but doesn't indulge my temptation. I probably feel more respect from her than anyone else I know."

Opposite-sex friends can be extremely valuable because they often help the struggling person challenge some of his or her perceptions of self. Andy reluctantly related to his friend Mary that "even if I wanted to be sexually close to a girl I know I wouldn't be good enough." Mary was wise and didn't just say "that's silly" or "how could you think such a thing?" She said, "let me tell you some things I admire and am attracted to in a man. See if you have any of these characteristics." He nodded and she continued.

"I like tall blonds," she said, "and I also like muscular men with dark hair."

Andy said, "Well, at least I'm blond and tall."

Mary continued her list. "I enjoy men who like music and art but I also tolerate the sports-fan type." Andy, who was now quite interested, said, "How about water color and tennis?" Mary mentioned many other things to which he responded.

Finally she said, "Now let me tell you what is the most important thing. I like men who listen and aren't afraid to show their caring. To me that is the biggest turn on I can have." He was surprised and later related that Mary's statement made him think for the first time in his life that he might be capable of being sexually arousing to a female.

GUIDELINES FOR EFFECTIVE SUPPORT

I suggest that the counselor consider the following guidelines in helping persons with same-sex preference to evaluate the support which they have.

1. How available is the person or persons to you?
2. Can you trust them to keep what you say confidential?
3. Will they challenge you if you are not being honest with yourself?
4. Do they understand the nature of the struggle?
5. Are they strong enough to handle the hurt the counselee feels?
6. Are they persevering enough to stay with the counselee, even through failure?
7. Are they capable of being close while keeping the relationship with the counselee nonsexual?

Although this list is not all-inclusive it will help you to guide the counselee toward the right type of people and away from some of the personal dangers.

Patterson and Eisenberg, discussing two reasons people have trouble changing, point out that (1) a change "feels unfamiliar and includes the risk of failure, no matter how logically it has been derived" and (2) "old familiar problem behaviors frequently have their own rewards along with the adversity they create."[4] While a new course of action may eliminate some negative aspects, "it may also reduce the rewards."

The support system within the church can make a contribution in each of these areas. For example, the support person or persons as well as the counselor can stand beside the person as he or she approaches the unfamiliar and takes the risk of failure. A good support system can also challenge the person to avoid the short-term rewards for the sake of the long-term goal. It is much easier to avoid the pleasures of sin when someone who really cares about you says, "You don't need it! Stay close to us. We love you."

As a counselor you can help build strong support for your counselees by being an encouragement to those who are providing their support. I recommend that you call them up and let them know how important they really are in the change process. Let them know that they are doing a good job. (Make sure you have your counselee's permission to call—it will build his or her confidence in you.)

You can also encourage your counselees to reach out to those who support them. It is not good for anyone only to take and never to give. Jill got hold of this idea and made it work with Marge, who was her support. She called Marge on the telephone and said, "When we get together this week I don't want to focus on me or my problem. I want to buy you a nice lunch and just enjoy talking with you." Marge later reported that the time had been helpful to her. She was beginning to feel pressure that it was her responsibility to fix everything for Jill. Jill's demonstration of normal emotional strength had taken the pressure away.

PROVISION OF SOUND TEACHING

In addition to demonstrating healing attitudes and providing strong support for the counselees, the church also needs to offer sound teaching. One thing I have observed is that persons who struggle with same-sex preference may get so involved in trying to solve their dilemma that they do not receive necessary input in all the other areas of their lives. When this happens—growth stops.

The sound teaching should not be limited to an understanding of homosexuality alone. The persons with whom we deal are whole people with other needs that are equally as great as their sexual struggles. Dan said, "One thing that has helped me the most was to realize that I needed to study the Bible to learn about all my needs, not just to look for new insights on my sexual struggle." Bill said, "I think it is a mistake to try to make our church teaching narrow in order to address special needs alone. We are Christians first and sexual strugglers second. Tell churches to keep the balance while trying to meet the needs of all special-interest groups."

When sound teaching is missing, counselees tend to sort through the same old set of ideas and never come up with anything new. This often leads to despair. I believe it is appropriate to refuse to work with counselees who are not doing good work for themselves. This includes involvement in good teaching and helpful reading as well as completing the assignments that come out of the counseling session. I ask them to keep a journal of what they are learning in each of these areas. Awareness of progress in these areas contributes to good counselee morale.

The counselor can help the counselee to evaluate his or her educational needs and to find sources that will help him or her to grow. Keep in mind, however, that each person is different and needs to be guided accordingly.

CHAPTER FOURTEEN

PUTTING IT INTO PERSPECTIVE

COUNSELING WITH HOMOSEXUALS. Is it for you? On the other hand, if you are going to counsel at all, how can you avoid this ever-present need among those whom you serve? Can you be helpful? Can anyone help? What does helping mean if your counselee does not want to change?

Many of these are the same questions you had when you opened the book. The topic of homosexuality is surrounded by confusion, and opinion that is rarely backed up with research. Does this excuse us from being involved, from caring, from learning? I think not! I believe as Christian counselors we have the responsibility to push forward into the unknown. We must read, we must learn from other pioneers in the field, and we must learn from our counselees.

How can you use what you have learned from this book? Don't put this book down as though you have completed an academic exercise. Rather, glean from it and begin to put your gleaning into practice.

Construct an assessment outline based on what you learned from chapter 8. Use the outline to guide you through the first two or three interviews with your next homosexual counselees.

Review carefully the chapter on specialized counseling techniques and practice those which are new to you but seem to have promise. Counseling skills are learned by practice. You have to try them out and see what feels comfortable to you. Involvement is the key to learning.

Think through the chapter on AIDS and decide how to develop your resource materials. Determine what impact you can make on your church in order that an atmosphere of ministry may prevail and that compassion may be shown to the stricken. Strengthen your skills on dealing with grief.

Find a friend or a colleague with whom you can share your fears and your doubts about your own counseling competence. Counseling is a very lonely field under the best of conditions, but when you are dealing with life-and-death matters it gets even worse. Don't try to be the Lone Ranger. You need your own support network just as your counselees and their families need to be guided to a support network.

Prepare yourself carefully with regard to the issues that result in the greatest arguments: biblical teachings and causality. I do not suggest this because I believe problems are solved by argumentation. I believe we need to be prepared so that we can be more confident within ourselves and so that we can adequately represent our beliefs when necessary. The issues are usually a matter of perception. You will do well to learn to ask questions to challenge others' perceptions, rather than trying to overpower them either biblically or logically. One man's whole attitude was turned around by one simple question: "What if you *do* have a choice?" Choose your questions carefully and keep your arguments to a minimum.

CONSIDER A TEAM APPROACH

As I stated earlier, I believe that the most effective counseling approach is for the counselor to be the same sex as the counselee. I take this position because I believe the homosexual condition is affected most by the relationship with the same-sex parent. The love and acceptance experienced in a counseling relationship with a person of the same sex can have a positive, curative effect by itself alone.

It may not be possible for you to have only homosexual clients of the same sex, but that is a desirable goal. I suggest you find an opposite-sex counselor or caring lay person who will work with you in order to insure that your counselees have the opportunity to relate to a counselor of the same sex. Teamwork is important.

After progress has been made in dealing with same-sex issues with your counselees it may then be desirable to have them work with a counselor of the opposite sex. John could not have worked with a female counselor at first. He was too hurt, bitter, and afraid. Initially it appeared that his issues were more related to his mother than his father. After a time, however, it became apparent that his feelings of detachment from his father were more critical than his hatred for his mother. He is ready to deal with his mother and I believe a female counselor can now relate to him and help broaden his views.

If you cannot offer a team approach the least you should do is encourage your counselees to open up same-sex friendships. I encourage my counselees to be involved with persons of the same sex in a nonerotic way in order to find out what true acceptance and friendship can be. Occasionally someone will call and say, "I'm John's friend but I'm really scared. I'm not sure how to relate to him." On some of these occasions I have related the situation to my counselee and asked for permission to talk to the two of them together. In these instances my counselee's friend becomes a part of the helping team. If the friend is too vulnerable sexually or too fragile emotionally I may suggest that they reconsider the friendship. In most cases, however, they are strong and eager to help as long as I can provide some guidance.

Opposite-sex friends may also become part of the helping team. They can reinforce the counselees' masculinity or femininity and let them know that they are desirable to the opposite sex. Most homosexual males, for example, don't realize just how attractive and appealing they are to females. Even though they may hate the "macho" approach they somehow believe down deep that if they were more "macho" they might be better males. This is not true.

Lesbians who have male friends need encouragement to experience their femininity. In some cases they believe themselves to be dumpy and undesirable to the opposite sex. Male friends can help by providing feedback and encouragement.

The treatment team for homosexuals is the total environment. If the environment shows acceptance and challenges individuals to keep their options open, healing will take place. I agree with Leanne Payne who writes,

Masculine and feminine can be understood only in terms of each other; basically they are opposite and complementary qualities, similar to darkness and light. It is very hard to understand darkness except in terms of light, and light except in terms of darkness. They are two extremes on a continuum. The masculine and the feminine within man and within woman, by whatever name they are called, or by whatever they are understood to be, seek recognition, affirmation, and their proper balance. Much that is called emotional illness or instability today (as I continually discover in prayer and counseling sessions) is merely the masculine and/or the feminine unaffirmed and out of balance within the personality. *Merely* is always, as C. S. Lewis has said, a dangerous word, and it surely is in this case if one does not recognize the potentially fatal blow an imbalance of the masculine and the feminine can wield, whether to the health of an individual, a society, or an entire civilization.[1]

ATTITUDES OF SUCCESSFUL COUNSELING

Two attitudes are essential if you are going to successfully counsel with homosexuals. These are patience and the willingness to deal with ambivalence.

One of the errors of Christian counseling is to suggest that the transforming power of Christ always comes in an instantaneous fashion and is usually associated with the awareness of and acceptance of new truth. Thus counselees are often told "If you just believe you will be changed." This is a half-truth. We must be patient. Homosexuality is learned and must be unlearned. Even though the desire for change may come about as a transformation from God, the process of change is often long and tedious. It is like building a wall. It must be done one brick at a time. In fact, it is like building a wall without a clear blueprint. You and your counselee may miss some directions. You may make some mistakes. You must patiently begin again. After failures counselees often say "What are you going to do with me?" I usually respond, "love you and send you back to find success."

I must also be patient with myself. If I try to reach my counselee in one way and it fails I need to try another way. I don't have to be perfect. I can learn from my mistakes and move on. I was refreshed recently by a counselee who said, "I've been thinking about what you told me about my relationship with my dad. I decided you're wrong." I cringed at first, as most people do when they are told they are wrong. After taking a deep breath I said, "Go on—tell me more."

He said, "I don't think you understand my dad or me very well yet. I don't feel that he hates me—I just feel like he doesn't know that I exist." I encouraged him to keep sharing and I realized that he was growing in his self-awareness by leaps and bounds. I patiently listened and the growth process continued. I realized that the mistaken interpretation may have been a blessing in disguise. I don't like to make mistakes, but the only critical mistake in this instance would have been to become defensive and try to uphold my point of view rather than listen to my counselee.

When you are frustrated and impatient with yourself it is advisable to talk to a friend or colleague who can help you evaluate or keep you on the path. When you are impatient with your counselees it is helpful to tell them that you get impatient at times. If you have a legitimate complaint tell them compassionately and tactfully. If they have a complaint with you, listen graciously and be teachable.

I experience ambivalence almost every time I work with a homosexual counselee. I wonder if I'm expecting too much. I wonder if I am expecting too little. I wonder if they are sincere. I wonder if I am sincere. I get angry when they don't change. I want them to give me something to write about. I become afraid when I see them playing with fire. I don't want them to get hurt. I admire their courage. I loathe their fears. I become afraid myself when working with them forces me to examine aspects of my own sexuality. At times I have said, "if this is so upsetting at times, why do I do it?" Then I listen to the answer from within: "You do it because you love and care. You do it because you can. You do it because God wants to bring healing to his people and you want to be a part of that healing."

Biblically we are challenged to be salt and light. We are told to restore gently. We are told to watch ourselves lest we also fall. Galatians 6:7 and 8 warn of doing things from our own sinful nature versus doing things "to please the Spirit." I used to think that the primary application of this passage had to do with lust, but I have discovered it is a warning against having a haughty or self-serving attitude as I seek to help people struggling with sin. I need to do what I do for God and for the person, not to make myself feel superior. I am no better than my counselees. We all have choices to make. Scripture encourages us to choose life. We need to challenge our counselees to do likewise.

Let us not become weary in doing good, for at the proper time we will reap a harvest if we do not give up. Therefore, as we have opportunity, let us do good to all people [especially the homosexual], especially to those who belong to the family of believers.   (Gal. 6:9, 10)

RESOURCES FOR DEALING WITH AIDS COUNSELEES

Agencies to contact:
United States Public Health Service Telephone Hotline
1-800-342-AIDS

National Gay Task Force
1-800-221-7044

San Francisco AIDS Foundation
333 Valencia Street 4th Floor
San Francisco, CA 94103

AIDS Project Los Angeles
7362 Santa Monica Blvd.
West Hollywood, CA 90046
(213) 876-8951

"Surgeon-General's Report on Acquired Immune Deficiency
  Syndrome"
U. S. Department of Health and Human Services
Hubert H. Humphrey Building, Room 725-14
200 Independence Avenue, S.W.
Washington, D. C. 20201
(202) 245-6867
This report has an excellent list of resources.

Local Chapters of the American Red Cross

State Departments of Public Health

Local Hospitals

Local Radio and Television Stations

All of the above sources have brochures and packets of material
they will make available to you at no cost.

NOTES

Chapter 1 The New Wave of Uncertainty

1. John R. W. Stott, *Homosexual Partnerships?* (Downers Grove, Ill.: InterVarsity Press, 1984), 23.

Chapter 2 Confronting Your Own Values

1. Carl R. Rogers, *On Becoming a Person* (Boston: Houghton Mifflin, 1961), 27.
2. Everett L. Worthington, Jr., *When Someone Asks for Help* (Downers Grove, Ill.: InterVarsity Press, 1982), 31.
3. Personal communication with DeLoss Friesen.
4. Gary R. Collins, *How to Be a People Helper* (Ventura, Calif.: Regal, 1976), 32.

Chapter 3 Biblical Controversies Regarding Homosexuality

1. Richard F. Lovelace, *Homosexuality: What Should Christians Do About It?* (Old Tappan, N. J.: Fleming H. Revell, 1984), 29.
2. Letha Scanzoni and Virginia Ramey Mollenkott, *Is the Homosexual My Neighbor?* (San Francisco: Harper and Row, 1978), 71.

3. Greg L. Bahnsen, *Homosexuality: A Biblical View* (Grand Rapids: Baker Book House, 1978), 14.

4. Rosemary R. Ruether, "The Personalization of Sexuality," in *From Machismo to Mutuality,* Rosemary R. Ruether and Eugene C. Branchi, eds. (New York: Paulist Press, 1976), 83.

5. Dennis Altman, *The Homosexualization of America* (Boston: Beacon Press, 1982), 187.

6. Robin Scroggs, *The New Testament and Homosexuality* (Philadelphia: Fortress Press, 1983), 7–16.

7. Lovelace, 35.

8. David Fields, *The Homosexual Way—A Christian Option?* (Nottingham, England: Grace Books, 1976), 5.

9. Scanzoni and Mollenkott, 70, 71.

10. Thomas Maurer, in *Is Gay Good? Ethics, Theology and Homosexuality,* W. Dwight Oberholtzer, ed. (Philadelphia: Westminster Press, 1971), 98, 100.

11. William H. Masters, Virginia E. Johnson, and Robert C. Kolodny, *Masters and Johnson on Sex and Human Loving* (Boston: Little, Brown, 1982), 346.

12. Don Williams, *The Bond that Breaks: Will Homosexuality Split the Church?* (Los Angeles: BIM, 1978), 47.

13. Ibid., 57.

14. Troy Perry, *The Lord Is My Shepherd and He Knows I'm Gay* (Los Angeles: Nash Publishing, 1972), 3.

15. J. Harold Greenlee, "The New Testament and Homosexuality," in *What You Should Know About Homosexuality,* Charles W. Keysor, ed. (Grand Rapids: Zondervan, 1979), 89.

16. Dietrich Bonhoeffer, *Life Together* (New York: Harper and Row, 1954), 54, 55.

17. Lovelace, 114.

Chapter 4 Causes of Homosexuality

1. William P. Wilson, "Biology, Psychology and Homosexuality," in *What You Should Know About Homosexuality,* Charles W. Keysor, ed. (Grand Rapids: Zondervan, 1979), 147.

2. Linda Murray, "Sexual Destinies," *OMNI* (April 1987).

3. Gary R. Collins, *Christian Counseling: A Comprehensive Guide* (Waco, Tex.: Word, 1980), 319.

4. *Homosexuality—A Psychoanalytic Study,* Irving Bieber, ed. (New York: Basic Books, 1964), 303.

5. Elizabeth R. Moberly, *Homosexuality: A New Christian Ethic* (Cambridge, England: James Clarke, 1983), 2.

6. Ibid., 5, 6.

7. Ibid., 19, 20.

8. Don E. Hamachek, *Behavior Dynamics in Teaching Learning and Growth* (Boston: Allyn and Boian, 1975), 111.

9. Earl D. Wilson, *Sexual Sanity* (Downers Grove, Ill.: InterVarsity Press, 1984).

10. C. A. Tripp, *The Homosexual Matrix* (New York: Signet Books, 1975), 82.

11. For a more detailed discussion of this phenomenon the reader is referred to chapter 3 of *Sexual Sanity*, "How Are We Aroused?"

12. Judson Swihart, *How Do You Say, I Love You?* (Downers Grove, Ill.: InterVarsity Press, 1979), 73.

13. John Money, "Sin, Sickness, or Status? Homosexual Gender Identity and Psychoneuroendocrinology," *American Psychologist* 42 no. 4 (April 1987):384.

14. Money, *Venuses Penuses: Sexology, Sexosophy and Exigency Theory* (Buffalo: Prometheus Books, 1986), 252.

15. Günter Dörner, "Sexual Destinies," *OMNI* (April 1987), 108.

16. Money, "Sin, Sickness, or Status?" 398.

17. Money, *Venuses Penuses*, 291.

Chapter 5 Lesbianism and Sexual Confusion

1. *Webster's New World Dictionary*, 2nd ed. (New York: Simon and Schuster, 1982).

2. Leanne Payne, *The Broken Image* (Westchester, Ill.: Cornerstone, 1981), 116.

3. Masters, Johnson, and Kolodny, 372.

4. John Money and Claus Wiedeking, "Gender Identity Role: Normal Differentiation and Its Transpositions," in *Handbook of Human Sexuality*, Benjamin B. Walman and John Money, eds. (Englewood Cliffs, N. J.: Prentice-Hall, 1980), 273.

5. William H. Masters and Virginia E. Johnson, *Homosexuality in Perspective* (Boston: Little, Brown, 1979), 65.

6. Masters, Johnson, and Kolodny, 162.

7. Ruth Tiffany Barnhouse, *Homosexuality: A Symbolic Confusion* (New York: The Seabury Press, 1979), 86, 88, 89.

8. Ibid., 89.

9. Dorthea McArthur, *The Birth of a Child in Adulthood*, manuscript in press.

10. Günter Dörner, "Sexual Destinies," 102.
11. Payne, 57, 58.
12. Moberly, 52.
13. Walter Trobisch, *Love Yourself* (Downers Grove, Ill.: Inter-Varsity Press, 1978), 14, 15.
14. Leanne Payne, *The Healing of the Homosexual* (Westchester, Ill.: Crossway Books, 1985), 32.
15. Barnhouse, 98.

Chapter 6 Special Counseling Considerations

1. Worthington, 130.
2. Sheldon Eisenberg and D. J. Delaney, *The Counseling Process,* 2nd ed. (Boston: Houghton Mifflin, 1977), 75.
3. Norman D. Sundberg, Julian R. Taplan, and Leona E. Tyler, *Introduction to Clinical Psychology* (Englewood Cliffs, N. J.: Prentice-Hall, 1983), 90, 91.
4. Hans H. Strupp, "Psychotherapy Research and Practice: An Overview" in *Handbook of Psychotherapy and Behavioral Change,* 2nd ed., Sol L. Garfield and Allen E. Bergin, eds. (New York: John Wiley and Sons, 1978), 5.
5. Robert R. Carkhuff and Bernard G. Berenson, *Beyond Counseling and Therapy,* 2nd ed. (New York: Holt, Rinehart and Winston, 1977), 151.
6. Worthington, 130.

Chapter 7 Assessing Counselee Needs

1. Phillip J. Swihart, *How to Live with Your Feelings* (Downers Grove, Ill.: InterVarsity Press, 1976), 19.

Chapter 8 Conducting the Assessment Interview

1. Moberly, 2.

Chapter 9 Helpful Models: Verbal and Visual

1. Paul Welter, *Family Problems and Predicaments: How to Respond* (Wheaton, Ill.: Tyndale, 1977), 212.

2. Antoine de Saint-Exupery, *The Little Prince* (New York: Harcourt, Brace, 1943), 67.

3. Worthington, *How to Help the Hurting* (Downers Grove, Ill.: InterVarsity Press, 1983), 119, 120.

4. Bill L. Kell and William J. Mueller, *Impact and Change: A Study of Counseling Relationships* (New York: Appleton-Century-Crofts, 1966), 39.

5. Ibid., 86, 87.

6. For example, see volume 3 in the Resources for Christian Counseling series, *Self-talk, Imagery, and Prayer in Counseling*, by H. Norman Wright (Waco, Tex.: Word, 1986).

7. Robert M. Gagne, *The Conditions of Learning*, 3rd ed. (New York: Holt, Rinehart and Winston, 1977), 242.

8. Kell and Mueller, 85.

9. Joseph Wolpe, *The Practice of Behavioral Therapy*, 3rd ed. (New York: Pergamon Press, 1982), 296.

10. Leonard Cammer, *Freedom from Compulsion* (New York: Simon and Schuster, 1976), 132.

11. Ibid., 220.

12. H. Norman Wright has provided many helpful suggestions for both relaxation and self-control in his book mentioned before (see n. 6), *Self-talk, Imagery, and Prayer in Counseling*. See also volume 11 in that series, *Counseling for Problems of Self-Control* by Richard P. Walters.

13. Samuel M. Turner, Karen S. Calhoun and Henry E. Adams, *Handbook of Clinical Behavior Therapy* (New York: John Wiley and Sons, 1981), 324, 325.

Chapter 10 Transference, Countertransference, and Other Key Issues

1. Gary R. Collins, *Christian Counseling*, 29.

2. Ibid., 40.

3. Moberly, 42, 43.

4. Ibid., 18, 19.

5. Collins, *Christian Counseling*, 273.

6. Roger F. Hurding, *The Tree of Healing: Psychological and Biblical Foundations for Christian Counseling and Pastoral Care* (Grand Rapids: Zondervan, 1985), 354, 355.

7. Moberly, 48, 49.

Chapter 11 Confronting Homophobia

1. Scanzoni and Mollenkott, 89.
2. Masters, Johnson, and Kolodny, 355.
3. Perry, 7.
4. Scanzoni and Mollenkott, 85.
5. Payne, 20, 29.
6. Scanzoni and Mollenkott, 94.

Chapter 12 AIDS, the Dreaded Killer

1. Duncan Grant and Mark Anns, "Counseling AIDS Antibody-Positive Clients: Reactions and Treatment," *American Psychologist* 43 (January 1988), 72–74.
2. "Safe Sex," American College Health Association, 15879 Crabb Branch Way, Rickville, MD 20855.
3. Ruth Mohr, "Deciding What's Do-Able," *The Family Therapy Networker* (January/February 1988).
4. Susan Holck, "Working with Families," *People* 14 (1987).
5. "AIDS in the Dawn of Fear," *U. S. News and World Report* (January 12, 1987), 60–70.
6. Ed Hurst, "Responding to AIDS" in *Outpost Newsletter* (1986), 1821 University Avenue, S., #5, St. Paul, Minnesota 55104.

Chapter 13 Mobilizing the Forces of the Church

1. David Atkinson, *Homosexuals in the Christian Fellowship* (Grand Rapids: William B. Eerdmans, 1979), 100.
2. C. S. Lewis, *The Four Loves* (San Diego: Harcourt, Brace, Jovanovich, 1960), 175.
3. Moberly, 47.
4. Lewis Patterson and Sheldon Eisenberg, *The Counseling Process*, 3rd ed. (Boston: Houghton Mifflin, 1983), 102.

Chapter 14 Putting It into Perspective

1. Payne, 45.

INDEX

Earl D. Wilson

Earl Wilson is a licensed psychologist and since 1983 has served as the director of the Lake Psychological and Counseling Center in Milwaukie, Oregon. He is also a professor of clinical and counseling psychology at the Western Conservative Baptist Seminary in Portland. Prior to that he was professor of educational psychology at the University of Nebraska for ten years. Dr. Wilson graduated from Multnomah School of the Bible and earned the M.S. and the Ph.D. in counseling psychology from the University of Oregon. He is a frequent conference speaker and has written seven books, including *Try Being a Teenager, The Undivided Self, Sexual Sanity,* and *Counseling and Guilt,* volume 8 in the Resources for Christian Counseling series. The author and his wife Sandy have three daughters and two sons and reside in Oregon City, Oregon.